MUSEUMS
OF THE ANDES

MUSEUMS OF THE

ANDES

Newsweek / GREAT MUSEUMS OF THE WORLD

NEW YORK, N.Y.

**GREAT MUSEUMS
OF THE WORLD**

Editorial Director:

Henry A. La Farge

MUSEUMS OF THE ANDES

Introduction by:
Junius B. Bird

Commentary texts by:
Elizabeth P. Benson
William J. Conklin

History of Andean Archaeology by:
Sergio J. Chávez

Photographs by:
Masakatsu Yamamoto

Design by:
Tsutomu Harada

Published by:

NEWSWEEK, INC.
& KODANSHA LTD. TOKYO

ISBN 0-88225-306-9
Library of Congress 80-8912

© 1981 Kodansha Ltd., Tokyo
© 1981 Masakatsu Yamamoto

Printed and bound in Japan
by Dai Nippon Printing Co., Tokyo

INTRODUCTION

Junius B. Bird
Curator Emeritus,
American Museum of Natural History
New York

Peru could well be called "The land of the unknown dead." Prior to the Spanish Conquest millions of people must have lived and died there, yet not one pre-Spanish grave is associated with a known or even a legendary individual. Rulers, heroes, priests, engineers, poets, architects, musicians, famous weavers and potters, goldsmiths, even accountants—i.e., the readers of the *quipus*, the knotted cord for counting—all are as anonymous as the least of their contemporary laborers or criminals. The same can of course be said of almost any populated part of the world prior to the development of writing and recorded history. But in Peru, with its abundant and impressive evidence of a long-established way of life, its complex and efficient irrigation systems, its religious structures, administrative centers, and defensive fortifications, the scarcity of knowledge about the human record and the people who lived there is particularly tantalizing. Oral accounts, transcribed after the Conquest, list the names of some rulers and people of importance, yet the details are meager and the related time spans not more than a few centuries.

Such knowledge as we have of the people of earlier times, as well as the details of what the legends report, derives either from archaeology and its supporting fields of scientific research, or from what the ancient artists depicted. Examples of what they produced are brought together in this volume, a sample collection drawn from various cultural periods and areas of Peru. It is not offered as a complete digest of what is available. Rather it will, I hope, awaken interest in, and appreciation of, the works of Peru's nameless pre-Spanish artists and people.

The objects illustrated are drawn from the collections of various museums, private and public. Over half are from the museum founded by that discerning and public-spirited collector, Yoshitaro Amano. He is an excellent example of what can happen. As he became aware of these things of the past, their diverse variety and their independence from the art of other world cultures, his interest, enthusiasm and understanding grew. In the end they led him to found the museum which bears his name.

As an archaeologist I am most intrigued by the possibilities of the desert coastal area of Peru, where preservation of perishable material must be witnessed at first hand to be appreciated. I have found flies at least eight hundred years old as perfectly preserved as if recently collected, and other forms of life up to four thousand years old have been recovered. Where such preservation occurs, at thousands of sites, there is little related to the life and activities of the people that cannot be rediscovered. Unfortunately, what is true along the coast does not apply to other parts of Peru.

The beginnings of serious archaeological work intended to achieve some understanding of the abundant prehistoric remains started less than a century ago. It had long been known that in the graves and tombs there was a widely varying array of ceramics, textiles and, occasionally, of copper, silver and gold objects. The first Spaniards to enter Peru were quick to learn that gold and silver could be found with the dead. They lost no time in exploiting the possibilities, and the profession of *huaquero* was initiated. A *huaquero* is a person who specializes in seeking and opening tombs for whatever of value they may contain. Originally it was a search for gold and silver, and that lust continues today, even though important finds of those metals are now few and far between. In the last century an appreciation of the ceramics and textiles started, so the *huaqueros* turned to saving and selling them to collectors. Others, who would not qualify as *huaqueros*, began seeking burials for curios. Some of these might go out only on All Souls day, as a pastime, for it was rumored that the dead came closer to the surface on that day and might be more easily found.

The result of all this is that the old coastal cemeteries, normally located on ground above the limits of irrigation so as not to waste cultivatable land, now resemble pockmarked battlefields. Skulls and bones lie scattered about in abundance until reburied by drifting sands; these were simply the remains of Indians, infidels—the fact that they were once human beings is forgotten. So callous have become some of their modern descendants that I have seen names spelled out in human longbones across the sweeping curve of sand dunes.

For centuries it was the practice to melt down whatever gold and silver came from the tombs. This has continued until recently for fear of confiscation of objects now protected by law. Not many years ago I was told by a man, who should have known better, of his disappointment when he and his men melted down a large cache of silver effigy beakers found at Chanchan: "When melted, they weighed practically nothing." What now saves such objects is not the law but the fact that their commercial value far exceeds the basic value of the metals. Deplorable as the commerce and traffic in looted tomb goods is, it has produced the bulk of the examples now in existing private and public collections. In fact, most of the objects illustrated in this volume were found by *huaqueros*. Unfortunately, for each item saved many more delicate, fragile and important things have been destroyed or abandoned. Equally unfortunate is the total loss of information about the association of items within individual tombs with the remains of men, women and children of which they were a part.

At most there may be general provenience data for objects so gathered, though only rarely can specific cemeteries or grave locations be identified. Everything else that one can say about any particular piece, how it relates to others in time and culture, is due to the combined efforts of Peruvians and others from many countries who have been concerned with the prehistory of the region. Chronologies based on ceramic styles have been established and the interrelationship to some extent deduced. "Cultures" have been named, generally with some geographical place name. As there are no rules such as apply to the naming of living organisms and their ancestral forms, there has been a certain amount of duplication and conflicting names have been given by different writers. With time, as pertinent knowledge increased, earlier designations, such as Early and Late Chimú, have been abandoned. "Early Chimú" may well be used, but it will have a distinctly different application. By the early 1940's there was a need for some better overall frame of reference than then existed to correlate what was being found in different sections of the country. One of the first to make a proposal that met with some approval was the well-known collector and amateur archaeologist Rafael Larco Hoyle. He saw the various cultural differences as, in part, evolutionary and in part influenced by the political or religious expansion of certain groups. Regionally this was a useful, workable system. Its weakness appears when applied on a broader scale.

Larco's proposals gave rise to various others, differing more in the terms used than in their application. One of the more recent, and the one used for the designations in this volume, was proposed by Prof. John H. Rowe. It is a simple, useful framework within which one can place or group the various cultural manifestations. The time brackets assigned the successive divisions are based on available radiocarbon measurements, subject to change and correction as better figures are available. Regardless of the problems of radiocarbon dating, the figures are far better than the earlier intuitive guesses at ages.

Rowe's outline of periods: Initial, Early Horizon, Early Intermediate, Middle Horizon, Late Intermediate and Late Horizon has one obvious weakness—it applies only to the record after the introduction of ceramics. This was deliberate and intentional, 11 but when the uninitiated see "Initial Period" at the bottom of a chronological chart the implication is that things were just starting. Some were, but only some.

The time of the first human presence in Peru is as yet uncertain. While radiocarbon measurements of extinct animal bones gave age figures of around 14,000 years and more, there are differences of opinion about the origin of the stone fragments found with them. That is not our concern at the moment. What is reasonably certain is that the first people were the late Pleistocene hunters of big game animals such as mastodons, utilizing whatever other food resources were available to them with the equipment they possessed. With the appreciably lower snowline then existing along the Andes, the associated zones of precipitation and desert were compressed. Rain fell in places which receive none today. Along the coast, desert conditions comparable to what one sees today must have existed, for within that environment evolved those intriguing, specialized plant species that make up the fog-nurtured *"loma flora."*

With the ending of the Pleistocene, snowline and precipitation retreated to the higher levels where they exist today, leaving reserves of subsurface water which must have played a role in the human record for many years. We do not know if the hunters who then occupied much of the higher parts of the country were descendants of the first people or of later arrivals. Their stone tools and weapon points have scant relationship to Paleo-Indian equipment elsewhere. That such equipment served its purpose is shown by wide distribution and the length of time in which it was in use.

In the later millennia of the pre-Initial or pre-ceramic times, population in the coastal valleys became sedentary. Hunting could no longer sustain life, and plant and marine foods became the mainstays. Settlements developed where food and water could consistently be obtained. One such community, the Huaca Prieta in the Chicama Valley, is marked by a mound of compact refuse still 45 feet thick after three thousand years of erosion.

No one knows whether the concept of agriculture developed spontaneously among these people or if it came from outside. Whichever the case, it seems certain that a limited number of plants were grown on land where water was available without irrigation. Among the plants either wild or cultivated was cotton. By the middle of the third millennium B.C. these Huaca Prieta people had a well-developed textile tradition, with cotton the primary fiber used. The artistic achievement one sees in the illustrations in this volume had its roots in part at least, in this early, pre-Initial period. In the fabrics of these people one finds truly creative art, which consists not merely of repeated motifs, but free figures of any given theme, limited only by the restrictions imposed by the fabric techniques. One motif, a serrated, double-headed snake, created about 2000 B.C., has persisted throughout the total record of Peruvian art and may still be found as a small detail in some modern Andean weavings.

Around 1200 B.C. pottery appears—earlier in some places, perhaps later in others. This marks the start of the Initial Pottery period. As there are also new plants, new textile techniques, new house forms, a population movement from elsewhere was obviously underway. There are some rather marked differences in the ceramics at sites of this period, differences still to be explained.

In due course another population movement was marked, in the Chicama, Moche and Virú valleys at least, by the simultaneous appearance of Chavín-tradition ceramics and the first maize and other plants. This was the start of the First Horizon, a period when Chavín influence, or religious concepts, spread over much of Peru.

No one knows what disrupted the seeming unity of the Chavín movement after it had existed for some centuries. In the Chicama-Virú valleys there was an abrupt break in the Chavín ceramic tradition with the appearance of what is designated as the Salinar culture. Their ceramic repertoire consisted of totally new forms, including whistling jars with strap handles and, in subject matter, the first erotica. The stirrup spout, so impressively modeled by Chavín potters, was not traditional with them.

Regionally the Salinar were followed by the makers of other distinctive ceramics utilizing resist decoration, the so-called Gallinazo ware. Similarly in other coastal valleys changes occurred on the same general time level. In the Nasca-Ica area one finds both stirrup-spouted water containers and vessels of Salinar form, both decorated in the Chavín style. These evolved slowly into a long localized sequence, the Paracas culture. A later phase of this was termed Paracas Cavernas by the famous Peruvian archaeologist Julio C. Tello, based on the type of tombs utilized. About the beginning of the present era a cultural mutation or cross occurred, culminating in the most elaborate and vibrant embroidered art produced in Peru. Tello called

13

this phase of the record "Paracas Necropolis." Later students see this as the initial stage of the Nasca sequence, for the mythical creatures, demons or deities of the Nasca tradition derive from it.

In the far north, in the region of Piura, the coastal Chavín ceramic tradition evolved into the early Mochica style, which spread south to occupy the Moche-Chicama valleys. Currently the name Moche equates with Mochica as a cultural designation, and is in common use: both are acceptable. In time the Mochica dominated or united the people of several valleys, constructing large irrigation systems and many ceremonial structures. Their art provides much information on the customs and beliefs of these people.

Comparable but distinctive records evolved elsewhere in Peru. It was this period of relative, regional independence that Rowe designates as the Early Intermediate. It began with the fading of Chavín influence and ended with the rather abrupt spread of the Huari, Tiahuanaco-related culture. Whatever the motivation, and it could have been conquest, this culture diffused over an area fully as great, or perhaps greater than that reached by Chavín influence.

Various archaeologists have worked and are now working on Middle Horizon problems: the record at the great center, the Huari ruins, the extent and nature of the Huari influence and its duration. Many more questions remain, principally with regard to what precisely was the relation between the Huari and the ceremonial center of Tiahuanaco.

With the decline of the Huari influence, or perhaps the end of political control, local autonomy revived, regional art styles began to appear and a new era—the Late Intermediate—made its appearance. In the former Mochica territory the Chimú, or Chimor, kingdom developed, with its last political center at Chanchan, near Trujillo. There were great and important centers of wealth and power in the valleys to the north at more or less the same time, and one would like to know how they were politically and socially related to the people of Chanchan. Whatever the record, all this changed abruptly when the Inca, starting from Cuzco, began their conquest.

14

In this last, relatively short epoch before the Spaniards arrived, the Inca achieved political control over a far larger territory than had ever been previously united. It was done by force and probably maintained by force. Certainly they did not gain the full loyalty of the people they controlled, which was one of the factors that helped the Spaniards when they arrived. The legends, mentioned earlier, relate to this period, the last or third Horizon in the Rowe chronology.

No thumbnail sketch of an involved and long segment of prehistory can be satisfactory to either author or reader. Intriguing detail must be omitted. Total lack of specific information creates gaps which cannot be filled. Quite naturally, one's thoughts turn to the possibility of continued research, to what could be brought to light. Again, one thinks of the continued destruction still going on. The laws of Peru made to protect their antiquities have been mentioned, yet as long as there are poverty-stricken men and others willing to finance them and to supply bulldozers, the lure of gold will lead to continued destruction—law or no law.

A possibly even greater threat to the archaeological heritage lies in the very practical problems Peru faces: a rapidly increasing population and a limited amount of arable land. The future will see irrigation greatly extended, using water shunted from parts of the eastern watershed and from storage systems in the mountains. Already areas outside the old irrigation systems are being flooded with water pumped from wells. I know an archaeologist who was refused permission from one governmental agency to study a midden relating to a little-known phase of Nasca culture who the next year found that another agency had approved an extension of irrigation on the land involved: the midden had been bulldozed, its wealth of plant material and thousands of textile fragments destroyed. It is unfortunate that the government has not created a national department of archaeology staffed by a corps of topnotch, professionally trained archaeologists, properly paid and with adequate financial support for their work, and, equally important, for the care of the material recovered. Such an organization will be worth whatever it costs; the return in knowledge of this remarkable country and its former inhabitants may well include information with a quite practical bearing on present and future problems.

Junius Bird

I Early Horizon Period

1400—400 B.C.

CHAVÍN CULTURE. *Temple at Chavín de Huantar.*

The most impressive and influential early Andean ceremonial center stands on the eastern slopes of the mountains, at 3,177 meters above sea level, next to the modern village of Chavín de Huantar, which gives its name to this early culture. The site lies in a small valley at the junction of two tributaries of the Marañón River, which flows into the Amazon. Passes through some of the highest mountains in the world lead to the western coast. The 15-meter-high temple was built, in several stages, with finely worked masonry of alternating large and small stones. The structure contains rooms, galleries, stairways, ramps, and air vents. Inside, offerings of artifacts—especially pottery—and animal bones have been found. The main portal can be seen in the center of this picture. The temple faces a large sunken plaza, visible in the foreground. The Chavín style spread widely over Peru; thus, it is known as an "horizon" style, and, because it was the first style in the Andes to have broad distribution, the period is called the Early Horizon.

Below right
CHAVÍN CULTURE
Temple at Chavín de Huantar, Peru
Ca. 850–250 B.C.

Below left
CHAVÍN CULTURE
Tenoned head, Chavín de Huantar temple
Ca. 350 B.C.
Granite; height 55 cm.
Temple at Chavín de Huantar, Peru

CHAVÍN CULTURE. *Tenoned head, Chavín de Huantar temple.*

p. 17

The temple at Chavín de Huantar was decorated with grotesque heads, carved in full round, with long tenons projecting at the back to be fitted into the temple wall. This one has round eyes, a wrinkled face, an upturned mouth with fangs, and an S-shaped ear. In a small cruciform room in the oldest part of the temple stands a tall lance- or prow-shaped sculptured idol. Most of the sculpture at Chavín de Huantar is not in the round, but consists of panels with incised or low-relief depictions of complex polymorphic creatures combining the attributes of human beings, felines (notably jaguars), raptorial birds (perhaps harpy eagles), snakes and possibly caymans (Amazonian alligators).

Facing page
CHAVÍN CULTURE, CUPISNIQUE STYLE
Stirrup-spout vessel with feline faces
Ca. 800–500 B.C.
Burnished and stippled black ceramic; height 22.5 cm.
North coast, Chicama Valley
National Museum of Anthropology and Archaeology, Lima

CHAVÍN CULTURE, CUPISNIQUE STYLE
Stirrup-spout vessel with "split" face
Ca. 800–500 B.C.
Burnished dark-brown ceramic; height 14.5 cm.
North coast, Chicama Valley
Rafael Larco Herrera Museum, Lima

19

CHAVÍN CULTURE, CUPISNIQUE STYLE. *Stirrup-spout vessel with feline faces.*

p. 18

Sites with Chavín-style architecture, sculpture, and pottery have been found on the coast north of Lima, across the mountains from Chavín de Huantar. This pot probably comes from the Cupisnique *quebrada* (gorge) in the Chicama Valley, a rich source of coastal Chavín pottery. Most of the finest north-coast pottery has a "stirrup spout"; this form endured in the north from pre-Chavín times until the Spanish conquest. Although the stirrup provides a handle, the spout shape is not very practical; it is possible that these elaborately decorated vessels were made only for burial. On each side of the bowl and of the stirrup on this example, a stylized feline face appears in low relief, with upcurving mouth, fangs, and snakelike hair.

CHAVÍN CULTURE, CUPISNIQUE STYLE
Stirrup-spout vessel, woman with child
Ca. 800–500 B.C.
Burnished dark-brown ceramic; height 22.5 cm.
North coast, Chicama Valley
Rafael Larco Herrera Museum, Lima

CHAVÍN CULTURE.   *Stirrup-spout vessel with "split"
face.*   *p. 19*

"Split" faces—a full face composed of halves of two different creatures or of
live and dead faces—appear in the art of the Andes and of Mexico. This
vessel has a characteristic Chavín deity face on the left, with a rectangular
eye, flaplike lid, and fanged mouth. On the right there is a monkeylike face
with two noses, and a snakehead at the ear. Monkeys, like jaguars and many
of the creatures seen most frequently on coastal and highland pottery, were
indigenous to the lowland rain forests of the Amazon Basin.

CHAVÍN CULTURE, CUPISNIQUE STYLE.   *Stirrup-spout
vessel, woman with child.*   *Facing page*

This vessel shows a seated woman, with strangely arranged hair, suckling a   21 child. The anatomical proportions are adjusted to make a capacious jar, which may have held *chicha*, a fermented corn drink. In early Andean art, representations of women with small figures are frequent, but the proportions of the small figures and the fact that they often have the haircut of a prisoner-of-war suggest that some depictions may not be mothers and children but oversize supernatural women with male prisoners who will be, or have been, sacrificed.

CHAVÍN CULTURE, CUPISNIQUE STYLE. *Bottle with incised head.* *p. 21*

Bottles of various shapes were common in fine Chavín pottery. The incised decoration here is like the incising on Chavín stone sculpture, but the rocker-stamped background is a typical early pottery convention. The design shows an upward-facing composite head with an enormous fanged mouth, a tongue, a snout, a rounded eye, an ear, a curving extension at the back, and pendant objects dangling below the chin. Like many other Pre-Columbian gods, Chavín deities were composed of elements from various animals that were thought to have special powers. Traces of red pigment are visible in the incising.

CHAVÍN CULTURE. *Painted tunic fragment.* *Facing page*

The Chavín culture reached its period of greatest influence about a millennium before the Christian era. The art of the culture was religious and powerful, and somehow found its way to the far corners of the land which we know today as Peru. Almost everything about the culture was revolutionary in comparison to the conservative traditions of earlier periods. For the first time, a single art style spread throughout a large territory, seemingly rather quickly, and that is why archaeologists refer to the result as the Early Horizon. As a cultural group the Chavín people brought not only great art but also great inventions to the rest of Peru, and textile painting was one of those inventions.

This fragment thus represents one of the oldest painted images in the art of the Western Hemisphere. Its symmetry is presumably a result of its having been created as part of a tunic, with the shoulder portion represented. The figure carries a snake-like staff in each hand and has snake-like hair under a skull cap. The mouth and eye are banded, and the belt has snake-like appendages. Fill-in images of hooked claws and pointed teeth surround the figure, which closely resembles images found as stone carving in Chavín de Huantar, a highland site many hundreds of kilometers from the locale of this textile. It seems likely that either the textile itself, or the idea for the textile, came rather directly from the highland site. The painting, originally in soft colors, was created on very fine plain weave cotton fabric. The painting style was highly influential, and for the next two and a half millennia, until Peru was conquered, Peruvian painters used the same techniques.

22

CHAVÍN CULTURE
Painted tunic fragment
Ca. 900 B.C.
240 × 56 cm. (size of entire fragment)
South coast
Amano Museum, Lima

23

CHAVÍN CULTURE
Mortar and pestle
Ca. 700–600 B.C.
Stone; height of mortar 7.5 cm.; length of
pestle 10.5 cm.
Northern highlands, probably Pacopampa
Rafael Larco Herrera Museum, Lima

CHAVÍN CULTURE. *Mortar and pestle.*

Corn, or maize, ground in a mortar with a pestle, was a staple food for New World Indians. The care and elaboration with which the objects seen here were carved suggest that they were made for special use. The mortar, or *metate*, is in the shape of a jaguar with circles indicating the pelt markings; there are stylized crocodile or serpent faces on the rim, and a guilloche, a characteristic Chavín design, on top. The pestle, or *mano*, combines a snake-head and serpent markings with fangs. Traces of red pigment—probably cinnabar, or mercuric sulfide—on the mortar may indicate that it was used to grind this ritually important substance, which was sometimes sprinkled on burials.

PARACAS CULTURE. *Embroidered mantle, detail*

Most religions have had a fascination with weightless conditions, with flying angels, with heavens, but rarely has the flying weightless condition been portrayed so perfectly as in this Paracas mantle. As the eye travels from one beautifully colored figure to another, their floating quality—their spatial tumbling—begins to move in the mind of the viewer.

The mantle was created by embroidery using the stem stitch in alpaca on a ground weave, probably also of alpaca.

Each of the figures carries a baton or spear in one hand and a fan in the other, and each has hair which gently streams in the breeze. The baton-carrying, horizontally-flying figure continues to occur for centuries afterward in Andean textile art, especially in the textiles of Tiahuanaco.

PARACAS CULTURE
Embroidered mantle,
Ca. 600 B.C.
261 × 146 cm. (size of entire mantle)
Paracas Peninsula
National Museum of Anthropology and
Archaeology, Lima

PARACAS CULTURE, OCUCAJE STYLE.   *Double-spout-and-bridge vessel with feline.*

The designs on this vessel—a full-face stylized feline with a polka-dotted profile body, standing on a guilloche band—are reminiscent of those on the mortar from Pacopampa (p. 24).   Chavín motifs are found on the south coast, but Paracas pottery is very different from that of the north.   Paracas designs are outlined with incising, and resin paint gives a distinctive lacquerlike surface.   The double-spout-and-bridge rounded vessel is characteristic of the south coast.   One of the spouts here is made in the shape of a head; the long black band passing through a rectangular eye is a motif also found at Chavín de Huantar.

PARACAS CULTURE, PARACAS NECROPOLIS STYLE.
Double-spout vessel, a basket of lúcuma.

Pottery in the shape of fruits or vegetables appears early in the Andes, possibly as a way of putting permanent "food" into graves. The bridged double spout indicates the south-coast origin of this attractive piece, which represents a basket of *lúcuma*, the edible fruit of a tree used for fine woodwork. One of the early writers on Peru, Garcilaso de la Vega, the son of a Spanish soldier and an Inca princess, describes *lúcuma* as a "rough fruit, with nothing rich or delicate about it, though it is sweet rather than sour or bitter, and there is no proof that it is harmful." Like the *achira* (Canna), it was commonly eaten in late pre-ceramic times.

Facing page
PARACAS CULTURE, OCUCAJE STYLE
Double-spout-and-bridge vessel with feline
Ca. 600–500 B.C.
Incised, resin-painted ceramic; height 17 cm.
South coast, Ocucaje (?)
Amano Museum, Lima

PARACAS CULTURE, PARACAS
NECROPOLIS STYLE
Double-spout vessel, a basket of lúcuma
Ca. 500–400 B.C.
Incised polychrome ceramic
South coast, Paracas Peninsula (?)
Regional Museum of Ica

PARACAS CULTURE. *Neck border from a Paracas tunic.*

The figures within this embroidered neck border are generally feline in form and have long wavy tails; but their most demonic characteristic is the proliferation of trophy heads. One is pendant from the demon's mouth, one from his tail, another hangs from one of his hands, still another is an earlike emanation from the top of the head. This terrifying creature also contains within the representation of his body a small version of himself. The glaring eyes of the faces transfix the viewer.

This neck border was originally part of a tunic which was undoubtedly largely of plain cotton cloth. The embroidery was created in stem stitch using alpaca on a cotton, plain weave ground cloth.

PARACAS CULTURE
Neck border from a Paracas tunic
Ca. 600 B.C.
47 × 21 cm.
Paracas Peninsula
National Museum of Anthropology and Archaeology, Lima.

NASCA CULTURE
Nasca painted textile, detail
Ca. 200 B.C.
68.2 × 252.5 cm.(size of entire textile)
South coast
Cleveland Museum of Art

NASCA CULTURE. *Nasca painted textile, detail.*

The painted figure illustrated is from an extraordinarily impressive, large painted textile which seems most likely to have been a wall hanging rather than a garment. The style of the painting is early Nasca, and a procession of standing mythological figures is portrayed, with the illustrated one being the most completely preserved. The figure is a mythical being in human form holding in one hand a human trophy head and in the other, a *tumi* knife whose use seems readily apparent. The figure also has a gold face mask, a forehead mask, and a spondylus shell necklace. He wears a sleeveless tunic (half of which is spotted) and a loin cloth, and has feline claws, face and tail. In spite of the evident attempt at ferocity, the painting also—perhaps ironically—conveys the appearance of a normal man in an elaborate costume. The technique of the painting is complex and fine line. Its quality, together with its scale, makes this perhaps the greatest painting left to us from ancient Peru. It was created at the height of the prestige and influence of Nasca art, which was a continuation and evolution from the earlier Paracas art. Painted Paracas textiles are, however, technically much simpler, and are essentially line drawings. The ground cloth is of cotton.

29

CHAVÍN CULTURE. *Vessel, seated man.*

Vessels in the shape of a human figure were common forms of elaborate pottery throughout the Andes. Utilitarian ware, of course, had simpler forms. This vessel, with an unusual rimmed, open spout, shows a seated man wearing a loincloth and holding a cup to his lips. Black and dark-brown pottery, without polychrome, was frequent at this time in the north, whereas polychrome pottery was common in the south.
The nature of Chavín power and influence is not yet understood; it may have been based on a combination of military, religious, and trade factors.

CHAVÍN CULTURE
Vessel, seated man
Ca. 850–250 B.C.
Burnished dark-brown ceramic; height 18 cm.
Northern highlands
Amano Museum, Lima

VICÚS NEGATIVE STYLE
Spout-and-strap vessel with animal head
Ca. A.D. 100–500
Red ceramic with black resist and white
paint; height 18 cm.
Far north coast
Amano Museum, Lima

VICÚS NEGATIVE STYLE. *Spout-and-strap vessel with animal head.*

One local art style that sprang up as Chavín influence waned was a black-resist-decorated style on the far north coast. Similar ware appears in the Virú Valley to the south. This vessel seems to combine the forms of an animal and a vegetable. The bosses on the back suggest that the creature may be an iguana. Plants and animals were sometimes combined in Andean art either to indicate the spirit of the plant or to merge creatures that had beneficial significance, although this may be simply a shorthand depiction of an animal eating a vegetable, perhaps a squash.

PARACAS CULTURE. *Double-cloth frontal figure.*

This standing figure from the Paracas religious repertoire is in outline almost straightforwardly anthropomorphic. But not in detail, for he has an upside-down image of himself contained within his body outlines, his hair is represented as snakes, and a reflected image of his own face appears above his head. At either side of his legs are cats. Within adjacent rectangles are repeated self images, each with snake hair and side cats. Two elaborate snakes frame the entire scene.

The textile technique is like a line drawing, and closely resembles Paracas line paintings, but has been created by a weaving construction called double-cloth. Two complete plain weaves, one of brown cotton and one of white cotton are woven simultaneously, interpenetrating in such a way that a white figure against a brown background appears on one side, and a brown figure against a white appears on the other side. The construction technique is one which continued for thousands of years afterwards in Peru.

PARACAS CULTURE
Double-cloth frontal figure
Ca. 600 B.C.
208 × 65.5 cm. (size of complete piece)
Ocucaje (?)
Private collection

PARACAS CULTURE. *Embroidered mantle.*

Paracas mantles are the most dazzling of ancient Peruvian textiles—dazzling both for their technique and for their art. Their clarity brings the viewer into immediate confrontation with the images of a deeply religious and demonic culture. The mantles have two broad style classifications—the color-area style, and the linear style. This is a portion of a mantle which is a superb example of the linear style. Scholars have pointed out that in the linear style, the bodies of figures have the same colors as the backgrounds, as if to make the images transparent or bodiless. Other scholars have observed that the images in the linear style seem to be constant from generation to generation. In this instance, the linear style image of double-headed snakes might possibly represent the name of a family or clan.

Technically, the images are created by embroidery in stem stitch using alpaca threads on a plain weave ground fabric. The colored areas are solid embroidery.

PARACAS CULTURE
Embroidered mantle
Ca. 600 B.C.
260 × 155 cm. (size of entire mantle)
Paracas Peninsula
National Museum of Anthropology and
Archaeology, Lima.

PARACAS CULTURE. *Tunic neck border.*

This neck border is from a Paracas tunic which was of plain weave. The border is in the color-area style, in which the figures are represented by color areas set against a neutral background. The figures all carry pointed spears and also carry fans. Viewed from any direction, half of the figures are always upside down, and adjacent to each is a miniature self-image which is always upside down to these main figures. Perhaps the artist's reference is to floating or flying. The exaggerated eyes, hair and mouths, as well as the luminous colors, give the textile a ghostly, spooky aura, but the meaning of the figures is not understood. The construction technique is the same as that used in the linear style; that is, alpaca stem stitch embroidery on plain weave.

PARACAS CULTURE
Tunic neck border
Ca. 600 B.C.
49 × 21 cm.
Paracas Peninsula
National Museum of Anthropology and
Archaeology, Lima

II   Early Intermediate Period

400 B.C.—A.D. 500

The religious content of Chavín art continued to influence the artists of succeeding generations, but whatever political power it represented waned, and the following period, known to archaeologists as the Early Intermediate, is characterized by the distinct art styles of regional powers.   One of the best-known and finest of these is the Mochica style, found in the coastal valleys of northern Peru.

MOCHICA CULTURE.   *Stirrup-spout vessel, seated man.*   *Facing page*

This early Mochica vessel represents a seated man with closed eyes and folded arms.   A woven coca bag is held on his shoulder by a rope around the neck. Throughout the history of Peru, coca leaves have been chewed, especially in the mountains where the coca counteracts the effects of altitude.   Pottery representations indicate that, on the north coast, coca was chewed ritually and in association with war.   The cap and the broad stripe on the garment seen here are associated with the coca ritual.   Mochica faces frequently have painted designs; this one has three circles.   Eyelashes and hair are carefully incised.   Although facial hair is not prominent on Indians, some faces do have moustaches like this one.

MOCHICA CULTURE.   *Stirrup-spout vessel with battle and sacrifice scenes.*   *p. 38*

The bowl of this vessel shows one warrior hitting another with a club.   The falling warrior, elaborately dressed and with a painted face, flings his club, spearthrower, and spears away, but clings to his square shield.   In the modeled scene above, an enormous anthropomorphic owl warrior leans over two very small figures—a kneeling naked man and a crouching anthropomorphic fox holding a knife to the man's throat.   The anthropomorphic owl was the patron of warriors and the god of human sacrifice.   Warriors captured in battle were sacrificed under the aegis of the supernatural owl.   This is a later form of stirrup spout than the example on p. 37.   Although the basic spout form remains constant, its proportions change through time.   These changes are one means of dating pottery.

MOCHICA CULTURE.   *Stirrup-spout vessel, mountain sacrifice.*   *p. 39*

Another kind of sacrifice took place in the mountains.   The Mochica people inhabited land that is one of the driest deserts in the world, except where rivers bring water down from the mountains. It was necessary for Mochica irrigation farmers to control water sources high up in the river valleys. This scene may depict a sacrifice made to insure a water supply. At the left, a seated deity with feline fangs—probably a mountain god and possibly associated with a Chavín god—looks upward. A painted sacrificial victim falls like water down the mountainside. Another victim, shown in relief, lies below. Victims in these scenes come in pairs.

MOCHICA CULTURE. *Dipper with man's head on handle and back view.* *p. 40*

A frequent form for fancy pottery is the "dipper," sometimes called a "corn-popper," although its use is unknown. The form may be a stylization of male and female genitalia, for depictions of sexual organs—probably related to fertility beliefs—are common in Mochica art. Some dippers have a phallus on the handle end; this one has a human head with a kerchief headdress. They also often have elaborate scenes painted on the back. This one shows a hawk warrior at the right, clubbing a fox-tailed polymorph. The helmet of

MOCHICA CULTURE
Stirrup-spout vessel, seated man
Ca. A.D. 100–300
Orange ceramic with white and red slip;
height 18 cm.
North coast
Amano Museum, Lima

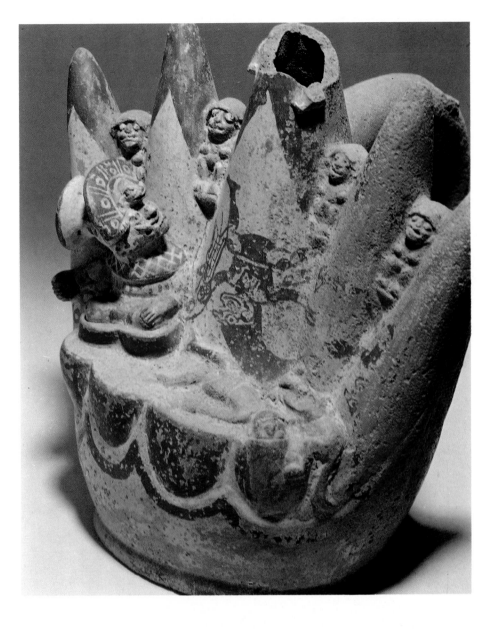

the polymorph lies at the bottom center. Around these creatures are small animals (possibly foxes), snakes, and a hummingbird; at the upper left is a bird with a human leg and arm, holding a club and a round shield.

MOCHICA CULTURE. *Open-spout vessel, seated man.* *p. 41*

This seated man wears a headdress with a feline head and upraised paws, a type of headgear often seen on warriors with coca bags. Ear protectors are attached to the headdress strap. The polka-dots on the shirt may represent sewn-on metal disks (see p. 51); the kilt is a characteristic man's garment. This is probably a portrait of a warrior-chieftain, for the face is modeled with care and individuality. Such portraits are frequent in Mochica art (see p. 45). Pottery was a major form of official art, for little stone was used on the coast, and the Mochica did not create monumental sculpture, as highland peoples did.

MOCHICA CULTURE
Dipper with man's head on handle and back view
Ca. A.D. 450–700
Red ceramic with red and white slip; height 29.5 cm.
North coast
National Museum of Anthropology and Archaeology, Lima

MOCHICA CULTURE
Open-spout vessel, seated man
Ca. A.D. 450–700
Ceramic with red, white, and brown slip;
height 46 cm.
North coast
Amano Museum, Lima

PARACAS CULTURE. *Ocucaje tunic.*   *Facing page*

This alpaca tunic is one of a group of tunics found in graves in the Hacienda Ocucaje of the Ica Valley in southern Peru. Ocucaje is near Paracas and is considered part of the Paracas culture even though the style of the material is slightly independent. The pattern on the tunic is commonly called a guilloche, but it is reasonable to see the intertwining, stepped lines of the design as representing a pair of intertwining threads. The great importance of textile construction to the people of Paracas and their absorption in the technology of weaving makes such an interpretation possible.

Like the pattern of the design, the tunic is constructed using a double-plyed thread. The tunic was not woven on a loom, but was made by simple looping, a technique which was even then 2,000 years old. The fringe is probably vicuña.

Facing page
PARACAS CULTURE
Ocucaje tunic
Ca. A.D. 100
82 × 76 cm.
Ocucaje
Obara-ryū Art Reference Museum

MOCHICA CULTURE. *Stirrup-spout vessel with "weapons bundle."*

A delicate-spouted vessel from the middle period of Mochica art shows a painted "weapons bundle," composed of a round shield, a warclub with the

MOCHICA CULTURE
Stirrup-spout vessel with "weapons bundle"
Ca. A.D. 300–450
Ceramic with white and brown slip;
height 24 cm.
North coast
Amano Museum, Lima

MOCHICA CULTURE
Stirrup-spout vessel, battle scene
Ca. A.D. 300–600
Orange ceramic with red and tan slip;
height 21 cm.
North coast
National Museum of Anthropology and
Archaeology, Lima

hitting end in the form of a human head, and two crossed spears. The shield
has spiral designs that may represent sun rays. The design is flanked by
hummingbirds. Small as they are, hummingbirds are aggressive and,
throughout the symbolic art of Pre-Columbian America, they are associated
with warriors (see p. 40).

MOCHICA CULTURE. *Stirrup-spout vessel, battle scene.*

Battle scenes are common in Mochica art, but most are shown in line drawings; this one in high relief is unusual. One warrior clubs another and, with
his left hand, grabs the hair of the defeated warrior, a sign of conquest. The
helmet of the vanquished man falls off to the left. The Mochica people conquered a number of the north-coast valleys and also fought the inhabitants of
the highland valleys. Scenes like this may recall actual glorious battles of

Facing page
MOCHICA CULTURE
Stirrup-spout vessel, portrait head
Ca. A.D. 450–600
Ceramic with red, tan, white slip and black
paint; height 28.5 cm.
North coast
Amano Museum, Lima

the past. It has also been suggested that they show mock battles that were part of a calendrical ritual.

MOCHICA CULTURE. *Stirrup-spout vessel, portrait head.* *p. 45*

Especially at one period in Mochica history, vessels took the form of portrait heads or full figures of individuals with recognizable features and often identifying scars. The same man may be seen depicted on many different vessels. Little is known of Mochica political structure, but these are surely chieftains. This man wears a characteristic cloth headdress with feathers painted on it. His face paint is unusual, but many Mochica depictions show carefully painted eyebrows. He has tubular ear ornaments and a necklace like that seen on the figure on p. 41. The necklace is made of *espingo* seeds from the Amazon Basin, which are used today on the coast for folk curing.

MOCHICA CULTURE.   *Stirrup-spout vessel, spiral ramp with temple.*

p. 46

A procession of foxes is painted on the walls of a ramp going up a pyramid or hill, and the pathway is lined with modeled land snails. At the top stands a structure similar to modern coastal houses that are made of *algarroba*-wood posts supporting a slanting roof of thatch or reeds. Rain is rare in the warm Peruvian desert, so shelters are often simple. Pottery vessels have also been found that depict houses of adobe brick, a building material widely employed, even for major architectural structures. For example the Pyramid, or *Huaca*, of the Sun at the site of Moche is the largest adobe structure in the New World. Some vessels of the type shown here show a figure—often a supernatural being—in the temple; but here the structure is uninhabited, indicating that the building and the hill themselves are sacred. The Andean Indians thought of many places—structures, hills, caves, etc.—as sacred abodes, or *huacas*.

MOCHICA CULTURE
Stirrup-spout vessel, woman with tumpline
Ca. A.D. 450–700
Orange ceramic with white and red slip
North coast
Amano Museum, Lima

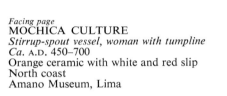

MOCHICA CULTURE
Stirrup-spout vessel, deity with Muscovy duck (?)
Ca. A.D. 450–600
Ceramic with red and white slip; height 26 cm.
North coast
Amano Museum, Lima

MOCHICA CULTURE.   *Spouted vessel, blind drummer.*   *p. 47*

This blind drummer is probably suffering from a disfiguring disease. People with physical handicaps were considered to have special magical abilities. The man's simple garments are of a type worn by priests who have duties in funerary preparations. Musical instruments also have associations with death. Drums are among the most commonly depicted instruments in Peru; others are trumpets (straight or recurved, often made of clay), flutes (see p. 98), and panpipes (see pp. 69, 99). This vessel has an unusual spout.

MOCHICA CULTURE.   *Stirrup-spout vessel, woman with tumpline.*   *Facing page*

This detail of a vessel shows a woman leaning forward as she carries a load on her back by means of a tumpline over her brow. Her raised hand steadies

49

the tumpline. This was a common way of carrying goods in the Andes. Pre-Columbian peoples did not use wheeled vehicles, nor did they have draft or pack animals. In the Andes, llamas were used for light loads—up to about 100 pounds—but many loads were carried by people in this fashion.

MOCHICA CULTURE. *Stirrup-spout vessel, deity with Muscovy duck (?)* *p. 49*

Little is known of Mochica deities, but one frequently depicted figure has a combination of the following attributes: feline canines, or fangs; a round eye; a wrinkled face; snakehead ear ornaments; and a belt appendage that ends in a snakehead (which is not visible in this photograph; it is at the end of the striped-and-dotted panel that comes down from the waist). The shirt with a bertha and a jagged edge over the loincloth are also characteristic. All figures that have these attributes and are shown in action may represent the same culture-hero god. Here the deity holds a knife, which has a snake— or a long cord ending in a snakehead—attached to it. In the other hand, he holds the head of what may be a Muscovy duck with its bill viewed from the top. When seen with this bird, the deity usually has insect wings. The same, or a similar deity, without wings, is often seen fighting a fish- or a crab-monster.

MOCHICA CULTURE
Stirrup-spout vessel, head of a feline
Ca. A.D. 450–700
Ceramic with white and red slip; height 29 cm.
North coast
Amano Museum, Lima

Facing page
MOCHICA CULTURE
Stirrup-spout vessel, kneeling anthropomorphic deer
Ca. A.D. 450–700
Ceramic with white and red slip; height 27.3 cm.
North coast
National Museum of Anthropology and Archaeology, Lima

MOCHICA CULTURE. *Stirrup-spout vessel, head of a feline.* *p. 50*

This powerful "portrait" head of a snarling feline is made with elegant realistic detail. Some Mochica pots were made basically in a mold; others, like this one, were hand-modeled. The vessels have great variety in shape. This is probably a puma, rather than a jaguar. All large felines had a special mystique, as they have had for many peoples in the world. They are, like man, hunters and meat-eaters; they are nocturnal and, in many regions, associated with caves and with the Underworld. Feline canines are often added to polymorphic creatures in Mochica art as a sign of supernatural power. Large felines are probably ancestral totemic figures.

NASCA CULTURE
Warp-weft interlock mantle
Ca. A.D. 400
200 × 80 cm. (size of entire piece)
Ica Valley
Amano Museum, Lima

MOCHICA CULTURE
Stirrup-spout vessel, pecten shell
Ca. A.D. 450–600
Ceramic with white and brown slip; height
20 cm.
North coast
Amano Museum, Lima

MOCHICA CULTURE.   *Stirrup-spout vessel, kneeling*
anthropomorphic deer.   *p. 51*

Deer appear on many vessels.   Some of the most elaborate scenes in Mochica
art illustrate deer-hunts, which must have had great ritual significance.
Many modeled pots depict realistic deer.   Other vessels, like this deer-headed
warrior, kneeling on one knee and holding a club, probably show supernatural beings, although this may represent a man wearing a deer-head mask.
Human warriors are seen in the same pose, wearing the same clothing—a
kilt and a shirt with metal disks, both bordered with metal plaques.   There
are often parallel representations with human figures and with anthro-
pomorphs or animal imitators.   Anthropomorphic deer also appear as
prisoners.

NASCA CULTURE.   *Warp-weft interlock mantle.*   *Facing page*

The color intensity in this textile occurs because both the warp and weft,
within a given part of the design, are of the same color.   Each of the areas
of the design is, in effect, a separate piece of cloth which has its edges interlocked with the adjacent parts.   The technique is one which had a very long
history, but pieces such as this one in a late Nasca style are among the most
brilliant ever produced.   53

MOCHICA CULTURE. *Stirrup-spout vessel, pecten
shell.*   *p. 53*

This beautiful pecten is typical of a category of Mochica vessels that represent recognizable species of animals and plants. The "realism" of Mochica
art has often been noted, but the frequent combination of naturalistic motifs
in ways that seem to us fantastic suggests that even pieces like this have other
levels of meaning. Probably even naturalistic art had religious significance.
Many of the realistic vessels show sea creatures, for the sea was of critical
importance to the livelihood of the Mochica.

MOCHICA CULTURE. *Bowl with men poling a reed raft.*

A rare pottery form, this bowl, when full of liquid, makes the reed raft appear
to float. Rafts like this, called *caballitos,* "little horses," are still made on
the north coast from tied bundles of tortora reeds. Ancient fishermen used
them; today they serve as dinghies for fishing boats or for sport at the

MOCHICA CULTURE
Bowl with men poling a reed raft
Ca. A.D. 450–700
Ceramic with red and white slip;
height 16.5 cm.
North coast
Amano Museum, Lima

water's edge. The cold, deep Humboldt Current makes the Peruvian coast normally one of the world's richest fishing grounds. This current, causing sea moisture to condense offshore, is one of the reasons for the desert conditions of the coastal land. The figures in this raft, wearing a two-pronged headdress typical of Mochica fishermen, are human beings; similar rafts with a snakehead at the bow and at the stern, are poled by deities (see p. 86). Because the sun sank into the western sea at evening, the sea was probably thought of as the entrance to the Underworld; certainly it was a supernatural realm.

MOCHICA CULTURE. *Stirrup-spout vessel with anthropomorphic bat.*

Many representations of pottery appear on Mochica pottery, for pots were significant and sacred objects. Various shapes are depicted on the bowl of this vessel, possibly representing the contents of a tomb. A drawing of an anthropomorphic bat is seen at the right. The "deck figure" is also an anthropomorphic bat, holding two vessels. Bats are often shown with pottery.

MOCHICA CULTURE
Stirrup-spout vessel with anthropomorphic bat
Ca. A.D. 450–700
Ceramic with white and red slip;
height 23 cm.
North coast
National Museum of Anthropology and Archaeology, Lima

CHIMÚ CULTURE. *Early Chimú tapestry.*   *Facing page*

This fragment of tapestry contains the representation of a very complex mythological scene, full of hints about the Chimú culture. The main figure, which faces us and is wearing a striped headdress array, is portrayed on a small platform in front of a temple porch which has a diamond-patterned roof. The temple has side wings, which also have diamond-patterned roofs. The central figure wears a tunic with three varieties of weaving patterns represented within it, and wears as a special neckpiece a double-headed serpent, and a scarf with large tassels. On the very right edge of the textile, a portion of an "X" shaped vertical loom is represented, with several bobbins below it. On the left side of the textile, two helpers are represented, one holding a bobbin.

Because of all the textile construction imagery, it seems reasonable to view this representation as that of a mythological figure which is associated with weaving. The textile itself, though not of fine construction, is of slit tapestry with twined weft reinforcing in the open work—a most unusual construction. The weft is alpaca and the warp is cotton.

MOCHICA CULTURE. *Supernatural animal.*

Gold had been worked in Chavín times, but Mochica metalworkers had extraordinary skill and inventiveness. They used gold, copper, and silver to make ornaments, and copper was used for tools and weapons, although many implements were also made of stone. This animal is constructed of soldered pieces of cut sheet gold with hammered, repoussé, and braided ornamentation and suspended cut-gold danglers. Inlays were used by goldsmiths, especially turquoise and chrysocolla, as in the eyes of this piece. The circles and fangs suggest that this is a jaguar, but its length may indicate a cayman or an iguana with a supernatural mouth.

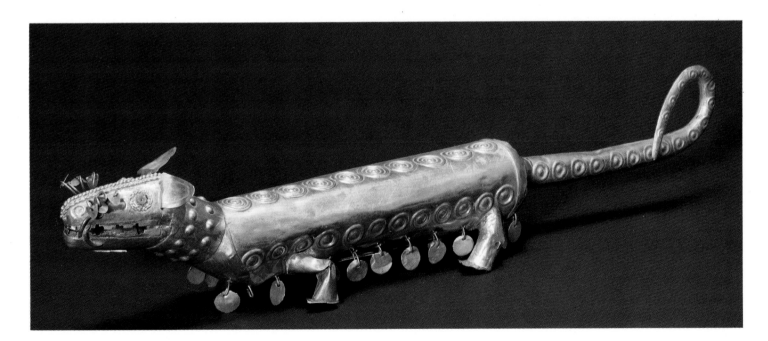

MOCHICA CULTURE
Staff or handle
Ca. A.D. 450–700
Wood with shell inlay
North coast
National Museum of Anthropology and
Archaeology, Lima

Facing page
MOCHICA CULTURE
Staff, and detail right
Ca. A.D. 450–700
Wood with shell inlay; length 1.74 m.
North coast, Viru Valley, Huaca de la Cruz
National Museum of Anthropology and
Archaeology, Lima

MOCHICA CULTURE. *Staff or handle*.

This fierce deity head may have been held as a kind of scepter, or it may have fitted into something. It represents the most important god in Mochica religion. His face is wrinkled, like that of an old man; the mouth is fanged; and the round, staring eyes may derive from those of a raptorial bird. The headdress depicts a jaguar whose body seems to have been split, for the rear legs are seen at both sides. Only deities and people of great importance—possibly deity imitators—might wear a jaguar headdress. This god is undoubtedly the same one shown on p. 59. He was possibly thought of as an ancestral deity, going back to the Chavín culture. There is no evidence of a direct link between the Mochica and the Chavín people, but it is clear that the Mochica wanted to be associated with that great power of the past. Many

58

motifs in Mochica art have Chavín antecedents, and sometimes Mochica potters made deliberate imitations of Chavín vessels.

MOCHICA CULTURE. *Staff.*

This long staff is made of the wood of the *algarrobo*, one of the few trees to grow on the north coast. Used in the past for structural material, it also provides shade, fencing, and animal fodder; its bean is edible. At the top of the staff stands a supernaturally-scaled deity wearing a hemispherical headdress with a jaguar head. One of his two snakehead belt projections can be seen at the lower right of the detail view. He holds a snakeheaded pole, under which stands a small figure. This staff is one of three found in the richest Mochica burial yet excavated archaeologically, the "Tomb of the Warrior Priest." A sacrificed boy was found next to the main body in the burial.

59

MOCHICA CULTURE. *Funerary gloves or replicas of hands.*

These hands undoubtedly come from a grave, but were not necessarily worn
by the corpse. In well-preserved mummy bundles on the south coast, gold
objects were found tucked between the many layers of garments that made up
the bundle. On the north coast, burials were usually made with the bodies
extended, and these may have been wrapped in cloth; but offerings were
normally put outside the wrappings. Hands had symbolic significance for
the Mochica. There are vessels in the shape of hands, and scenes on pottery
indicate that hands or forearms were amputated in ritual deaths. Gold
forearms are also found in the grave goods of the later Chimú culture.

MOCHICA CULTURE
Funerary gloves or replicas of hands
Ca. A.D. 450–800
Gold, cut and hammered; length 20 and
22 cm.
North coast
The Gold Museum, Lima

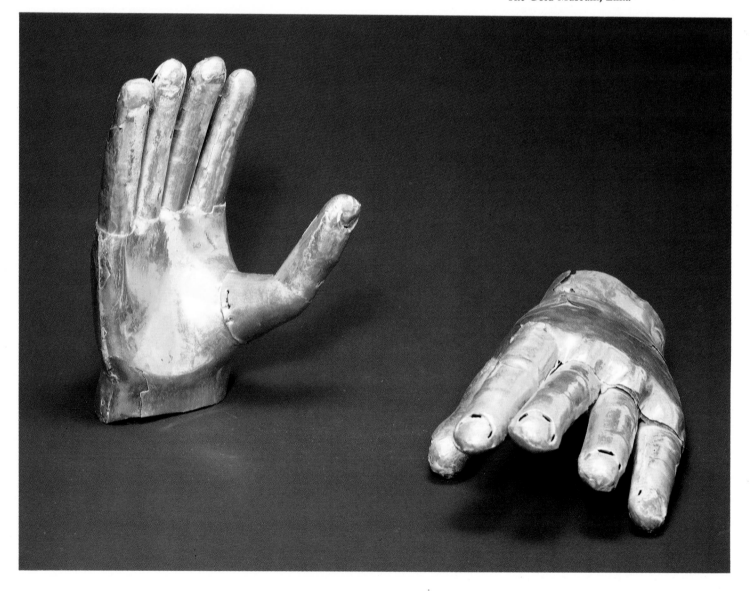

MOCHICA CULTURE
Nose ornament with two spiders
Ca. A.D. 450–700
Gold; diameter 2.8 cm.
Far north coast
Amano Museum, Lima

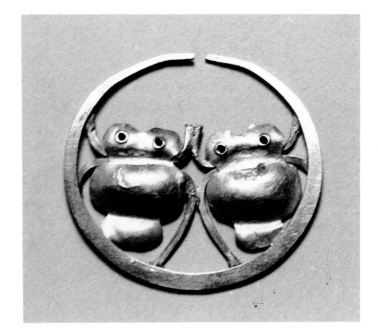

MOCHICA CULTURE. *Nose ornament with two spiders.*

Spiders are a frequent motif of the goldwork of the far north coast, but are rare elsewhere. The break in the rim of this disk fits around the septum between the nostrils. Such ornaments were worn by people of special status on specific occasions. A number of important gold finds from this period have been made on the far north coast, where the Mochica culture may have developed before it spread southward. These, apparantly, do not all come from burials; many of the objects seem to have come from caches, or hoards.

RECUAY CULTURE
Vessel with flaring spout
Ca. A.D. 1–500
Ceramic, black resist decoration and red
and white paint; height 17 cm.
Northern highlands, Callejón de Huaylas
Amano Museum, Lima

RECUAY CULTURE.   *Vessel with flaring spout.*

In the Callejón de Huaylas, a long valley in the mountains between Chavín de Huantar and the Mochica coast, a culture called Recuay (after a modern town) developed contemporaneously with the Mochica. Many Recuay motifs are similar to Mochica ones, but they are used in a different iconographic system. Mochica motifs are usually specific to a certain occasion, but Recuay motifs are seemingly more interchangeable. The vessel shapes are very different from those of the coast, and the pottery is decorated with resist (negative) designs. Here the head of a man emerges from the vessel, flanked on either side by a figure holding two cups.

RECUAY CULTURE.   *Spouted vessel, structure with*
figures and detail.   *Facing page*

This two-level vessel is composed of a lower boxlike form and an upper structure that is roofless to expose the three figures within it. The large central figure has S-shaped ears, a motif from earlier Chavín art (see p. 17). The headdress with raised ears is a form that probably came to coastal Mochica art from Recuay (see p. 41). This figure and a smaller one, probably a woman, hold cups, as if offering liquid or perhaps sacred pottery. The

62

RECUAY CULTURE
*Spouted vessel, structure with figures, and
detail above*
Ca. 100 B.C.–A.D. 500
Ceramic, black resist decoration and red and
white paint; height 20 cm.
Northern highlands, Callejón de Huaylas
Amano Museum, Lima

63

other figure is empty-handed, but there is a cup in front of it. A step motif appears on the walls. The major spout is fitted into this enclosure; there is also a small spout at the upper corner of the lower compartment. Both tiers have resist decoration, a frontal face that may depict a skull; this is also seen on p. 63.

NASCA CULTURE.   *Spout-and-bridge vessel, figure holding trophy head.*

On the south coast, the Nasca people were contemporaries of the Mochica. Like northern vessels, Nasca pots were often made in the shape of a human figure, but Nasca potters used more color, and Nasca design zones are often outlined in black. This elaborately dressed personage holds a human head. Ritual decapitation was frequent in Pre-Columbian America, especially in

NASCA CULTURE
Spout-and-bridge vessel, figure holding trophy head
Ca. A.D. 300–500
Polychrome ceramic; height 19 cm.
South coast
Amano Museum, Lima

NASCA CULTURE
Double-spout-and-bridge vessel with deity
Ca. A.D. 100–300
Polychrome ceramic; height 18 cm.
South coast
Amano Museum, Lima

the Andes. The head, as the most important part of the human body, may have been considered a valuable offering to a god, and/or its loss may have been the surest way of depriving an enemy of power. Sacrifice probably insured the fertility and continuance of the world. Trophy-head-holding figures, with crossed bands on the headdress, symbolic elements on a kind of cape, and what appear to be tie-dyed garments, are common at this time. These figures also have real or imitation facial hair.

NASCA CULTURE. *Double-spout-and-bridge vessel with deity.*

The double-spout-and-bridge and squashed globular form declare this vessel to be a direct descendant of Paracas pottery (see p. 26), but, instead of a resin-painted, incised-zone surface, the polychrome is smoothly applied. Pottery at this time is well made and usually decorated with three or more clear slip colors. The design is also still quite close to Paracas. The creature here has an enormous frontal head, and wears mouth and brow masks. Examples of such masks actually exist in cut-out sheet gold. The body and legs of the creature are seen to the right. Under his chin, he holds a trophy head by the hair. Other trophy heads are attached to the body.

NASCA CULTURE. *Double-spout-and-bridge vessel, animated squash (?)*

This four-footed vessel may represent an animated vegetable or fruit, possibly a squash. Facial features or limbs were sometimes added to show the supernatural life of a vegetable. Like the Mochica, the Nasca people were both farmers and fishermen, and their art is full of symbols of these worlds. Basic food crops were squash, maize, chili peppers, beans, potatoes, manioc (a root crop), and peanuts; cotton and gourds, for use as utensils, were also grown. Farmers planted seeds with a wooden digging stick. Crops were probably fertilized with guano found on offshore islands.

NASCA CULTURE. *Double-spout-and-bridge vessel with decapitation scene.* *Facing page*

This late Nasca vessel takes the form of a widespread Andean motif. The stepped-triangle-and-swirl was used from the Chavín era on. It was apparently imported into Mexico, where it became particularly prominent at Monte Albán, in Oaxaca. The meaning of the motif is not known, and may have changed through time and from place to place. The swirl may stand for the sea and the stepped triangle for mountains; the interaction of these two environments was of great importance to Andean peoples. An elaborate

NASCA CULTURE
Double-spout-and-bridge vessel, animated squash (?)
Ca. A.D. 100–300
Polychrome ceramic; height 13 cm.
South coast
Amano Museum, Lima

NASCA CULTURE
Double-spout-and-bridge vessel with decapitation scene
Ca. A.D. 300–500
Polychrome ceramic; height 13 cm.
South coast
Amano Museum, Lima

and violent scene is enacted here. At the left, a large enthroned figure in a jaguar-skin cape holds a knife in his left hand and the hair of a struggling victim in his right. (The shape of the vessel suggests that the enthroned figure is sitting on a stepped pyramid.) Two other figures in fur capes are also about to behead victims. All the headsmen wear shirts with sleeves. There are birds, probably harpy eagles, behind the two upper figures.

NASCA CULTURE. *Double-spout-and-bridge vessel, killer whale or shark.*

The creature depicted here has traditionally been identified as a killer whale, but it may be a shark. It appeared first on Paracas textiles; it is also seen painted two-dimensionally on the bowls of Nasca vessels. A tour-de-force of pottery-making, this open-mouthed creature holds a trophy head in one hand (or flipper); its back is scaled with trophy heads. The terrors that the sea held for coastal peoples are reflected in motifs like this.

NASCA CULTURE
Double-spout-and-bridge vessel,
killer whale or shark
Ca. A.D. 100–300
Polychrome ceramic; length 35 cm.
South coast
National Museum of Anthropology and
Archaeology, Lima

NASCA CULTURE. *Panpipes with birds.*

Among Pre-Columbian musical instruments frequently depicted in scenes on pottery are panpipes, which are usually associated with high-status figures. Actual examples, like this one, have also been found. Most panpipes were made of reeds of varying lengths tied together; pottery examples are rare, except in the Nasca region. This one has a red background and a design of flying black birds, which are probably white-collared swifts. These birds are frequently seen as a repeated design on Nasca vessels.

NASCA CULTURE
Panpipe with birds
Ca. A.D. 300–500
Polychrome ceramic; length 17.5 cm.
South coast
Regional Museum of Ica

NASCA CULTURE
*Double-spout-and-bridge vessel with flying
seabirds*
Ca. A.D. 100–300
Polychrome ceramic; height 15.5 cm.
South coast
Amano Museum, Lima

NASCA CULTURE.   *Double-spout-and-bridge vessel with flying seabirds.*

Seabirds, common in coastal art of this period, fly across this typically shaped Nasca vessel.   These may be red-footed boobies, tropical birds related to gannets.   The Nasca people created not only fine ceramics and textiles; one of their claims to modern fame is the series of great images they inscribed on a plain in the Nasca Valley.   These images, made by removing the top layer of earth, are sometimes birds, animals, or mythical creatures, and sometimes straight lines and geometrical shapes extending across the plain. These probably had astronomical-astrological significance, and may have been offerings to sky deities.   Birds like the ones shown on this vessel may also have been associated with sky deities.

NASCA CULTURE
Double-spout-and-bridge vessel, achira
Ca. A.D. 300–500
Polychrome ceramic; height 18 cm.
South coast
Amano Museum, Lima

NASCA CULTURE. *Double-spout-and-bridge vessel*, achira.

The striking form of this vessel represents the rhizomes of a Canna family plant called *achira*. Boiled, these edible rhizomes taste like an inferior sweet potato. They are still eaten today. Such vegetables play an important part in the Andes, for much of the land is at altitudes where little else will grow. Pre-Columbian potters did not use a wheel; they modeled freely or built up rounded forms with coils of clay.

NASCA CULTURE. *Double-spout-and-bridge vessel with deities and parrots.*

Mochica and Nasca potters used similar basic forms, like this "box" with deck figures. A pair of modeled parrots stands over what appear to be kernels of maize. The creature partially seen on the left face of the box has simplified trophy heads on a stylized wing. The creature in full view holds a staff. Probably the same long-tongued deity seen on p. 65—one of the most frequently depicted Nasca gods—it wears brow and mouth masks and a plate-metal collar. The body seems to be composed of sprouting plants, suggesting that this is an agriculture deity.

NASCA CULTURE
Double-spout-and-bridge vessel with deities and parrots
Ca. A.D. 100–300
Polychrome ceramic; height 20 cm.
South coast
National Museum of Anthropology and Archaeology, Lima

NASCA CULTURE. *Flaring-rim vase with hunting scene.*

This graceful late Nasca vase shows a nude hunter with a spear, as well as a number of spears flying through the air or piercing simply drawn deer. In other contexts, it has been suggested that circular forms like those seen here signify a night scene; but that does not fit this scene. The forms may represent fruit, for vegetation is seen in Mochica deer-hunt scenes. Deer were indigenous to the coast, and deer-hunting was surely both a ritual and a means of supplying food; the hunted deer was probably considered a sacrifice.

NASCA CULTURE
Flaring-rim vase with hunting scene
Ca. A.D. 300–500
Polychrome ceramic; height 17 cm.
South coast
Amano Museum, Lima

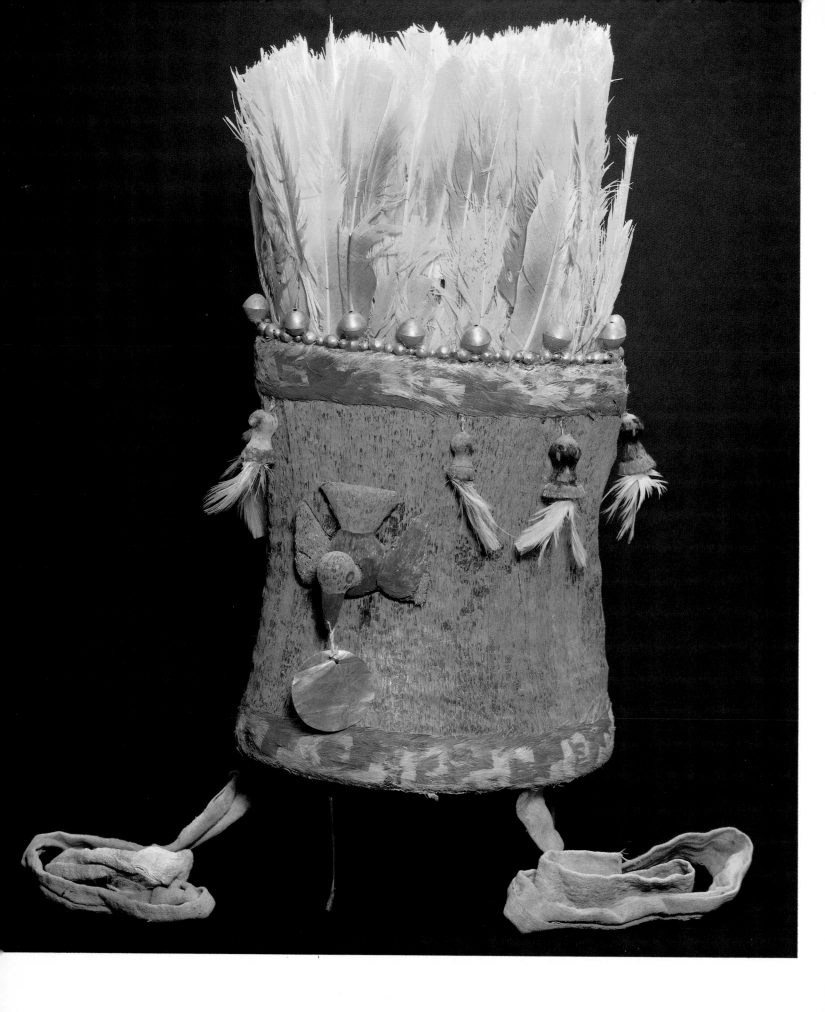

NASCA CULTURE
Feathered basketry crown
Ca. 100 B.C.–A.D. 400
Height 37 cm.
South coast
The Gold Museum, Lima

NASCA CULTURE. *Feathered basketry crown.*

When feathers are directly adhered in patterns without being individually attached by threads, the technique is called feather mosaic. Such mosaic work is relatively rare in ancient Peru, and little is known about its evolution over time. This basketry crown is patterned with very high-quality mosaic work of brilliantly colored tropical feathers. The step design in the feather work is an almost universal Pre-Columbian motif. The gold elements appear to be recent additions.

75

NASCA CULTURE. *Textile flowers and birds.*

Though somewhat difficult to fully perceive, this example of three-dimensional cross-knit looping is a portrayal of birds and flowering plants which alternate along the horizontal base. The birds, perhaps like hummingbirds, have their beaks in the flowers for nectar, with their tripartite tails extending below the base for equipoise. This fragment comes from that early portion of the Early Intermediate Period in the south coast when the Nasca culture was highly influential, when their textiles and pottery were at the height of their inventiveness and aesthetic brilliance. The subject matter, the nature scene of birds and flowers, contrasts sharply with the religious concerns of the preceding Paracas culture. Though the method of making this multicolored three-dimensional textile with dyed alpaca is not fully understood, it must have somewhat resembled crocheting.

NASCA CULTURE
Textile flowers and birds
Ca. 200 B.C.–A.D. 100
6.5 × 31 cm.
South coast
The Gold Museum, Lima

III Middle Horizon Period

A.D. 500—900

TIAHUANACO CULTURE. *The Ponce Monolith.*

The Middle Horizon is defined by the spread of Tiahuanaco motifs from the southern highlands to the west and the north. One of the great ceremonial centers of the preceding Early Intermediate period was at Tiahuanaco, near La Paz, on a great mountain-rimmed plain *ca.* 3,850 meters above sea level. It is a bleak, impersonal landscape, but men have lived there for millennia. Free-standing monolithic figures with low-relief decoration gaze out across the vast expanse. The hat or headband of this sculpture has a frieze of running figures, which are repeated in tattoolike incising on his torso, possibly imitating the decorative panels of a shirt, or poncho (see p. 93). A band around the eye ends in a snakehead. He holds two macelike objects, decorated with snakes.

TIAHUANACO CULTURE
The Ponce Monolith
Ca. A.D. 7th century
Andesite; height 2.8 m.
Tiahuanaco, Bolivia

TIAHUANACO CULTURE. *Gate of the Sun.*

A dominant feature of Tiahuanaco is the so-called Gate of the Sun, carved from a single block of stone. The upper portion is incised with a complicated low-relief design. Long after the great period of Tiahuanaco, the site was considered sacred, and was visited on pilgrimages. Various versions of later Inca creation myths refer to either Tiahuanaco or nearby Lake Titicaca as the place where the sun first rose or where the first Inca appeared.

TIAHUANACO CULTURE.
Gate of the Sun, detail.   *Facing page*

The central figure has a projecting, oversized face, like a mask or a shield. Appendages with serpent heads or circular elements radiate from it. A winged snake is incised around each eye, and the eyes were probably inlaid. Wearing a poncho or tunic of classic Tiahuanaco design and a belt with a snakehead at either side, and holding staffs terminating in birdheads, the truncated figure stands on a stepped platform. Flanking the central figure are small, running profile figures, some of which have birdheads. They all wear capes like wings, with snakeheads on them, and they, too, carry staffs. Staff-bearing figures, winged profile figures, and snakehead belts were also motifs in Chavín art. The motifs from the Gate of the Sun appear, with variations, on later sculpture, ceramics, and textiles all over Peru.

Below and detail right
TIAHUANACO CULTURE
Gate of the Sun
Ca. A.D. 400–700
Andesite; height 3 m.
Tiahuanaco, Bolivia

HUARI CULTURE
Tiahuanacoid tunic
Ca. A.D. 600–1000
105 × 210 cm.
Amano Museum, Lima

HUARI CULTURE. *Tiahuanacoid tunic.* *Facing page*

This fine tapestry tunic has been opened up so that the design of both the front and back can be seen at once. It is constructed of interlocked tapestry in two long panels which were woven separately. The design consists of winged figures, carrying staffs and wearing elaborate headdresses. The sixteen figures represented are in alternating colors of blue, pink, or tan against a red background, with the design bands separated by striping. These figures appear to be running or kneeling when viewed with the stripes vertical. As they were in the artist/weaver's loom, the figures are seen to be horizontal flying figures.

Flying deities seem to have been very important in the highland culture of Tiahuanaco, Bolivia, and their representation in various forms was carried over to the Huari culture of central Peru. The quality of the weaving and the nearly abstract representations of the deities make these highland tapestry tunics seem to be the most sophisticated and urbane of all Pre-Columbian textiles. The weft is alpaca; the warp is probably cotton.

TIAHUANACO CULTURE. *Open vessel with feline head.*

This distinctive "gravy-boat" shape is characteristic of the early or classic phase of Tiahuanaco art. Unlike the *kero* form, it is rarely found in later

TIAHUANACO CULTURE
Open vessel with feline head
Ca. A.D. 400–700
Polychrome ceramic; height 30 cm.
Bolivia, southern highlands (?)
National Museum of Anthropology and Archaeology, Lima

81

pottery. The open bowl makes it an uncommon way of forming an effigy vessel, but the general outline of an animal shape is incorporated. It may have been used for food offerings.

TIAHUANACO CULTURE. *Beaker, or* kero.

The beaker, or *kero*, is a classic Tiahuanaco form, which remained prevalent for centuries. Later examples were made in gold and in wood (see pp. 113, 158). The lower band of this one has a stepped-triangle-and-swirl motif; the upper bands shows a feline head at the left and a wing at the right. These are symbolic motifs that were important throughout the Pre-Columbian history of the Andes. Typical of this style is the feline head with fangs, made by drawing a diagonal line through a rectangle; it is a motif that appears frequently on textiles.

TIAHUANACO-HUARI CULTURE.
Urn with deity.   *Facing page*

The spread of the Tiahuanaco art style over the Central Andes was probably achieved by the aggression of the people of Huari, a site near the Peruvian highland city of Ayacucho. This large south-coast urn, with projections that serve as handles, features a deity very close to the one on the Gate of the Sun

TIAHUANACO CULTURE
Beaker, or kero
Ca. A.D. 400–700
Polychrome pottery; height 15.5 cm.
Bolivian highlands (?)
Amano Museum, Lima

Facing page
TIAHUANACO-HUARI CULTURE
Urn with deity
Ca. A.D. 700–800
Polychrome ceramic; height 33 cm.
South coast, Ica Valley (?), Peru
National Museum of Anthropology and Archaeology, Lima

at Tiahuanaco (see p. 79). A frontal, staff-holding figure with a masklike face, it has simplified bird forms surrounding the eye; but the radiances around the head of the Tiahuanaco figure have been replaced with feathers, and snake images have disappeared. The heads around the top rim, inside and outside, have hanks of hair, and probably represent trophy heads.

TIAHUANACO-HUARI CULTURE, ROBLES MOQO STYLE. *Huge vessel with mask face.*

Extremely large decorated vessels appear at this time, attesting to mastery of the potter's craft; earlier large vessels had been simple and utilitarian, used for food storage or perhaps for the burial of children. This one, derived from the Tiahuanaco *kero* form, mingles highland and local south-coast motifs. The masklike face in high relief derives from the one on the Gate of the Sun. It is embellished with knife-shaped ornaments with faces on the

TIAHUANACO-HUARI CULTURE, ROBLES MOQO STYLE
Huge vessel with mask face
Ca. A.D. 700–800
Polychrome ceramic; height 60 cm.
South coast, Nasca Valley, Pacheco, Peru
National Museum of Anthropology and Archaeology, Lima

TIAHUANACO-HUARI CULTURE
Spouted vessel, llama
Ca. A.D. 700–800
Polychrome ceramic; height 70 cm.
South coast, Nasca Valley, Pacheco
National Museum of Anthropology and
Archaeology, Lima

blades; a plant grows from the top of each buttonlike eye. The design of plants around the rim derives from Nasca art. There was an Andean convention of showing plants with their roots. The fret design is made in an unusual way, but both it and the rectangles with circles are pan-Andean motifs; the latter probably indicate a garment of metal plates.

TIAHUANACO-HUARI CULTURE. *Spouted vessel, llama.*

From Chavín times onward, vessels were made in the shape of animals; but this one is of exceptional size. The spout is made to look like a vessel resting on the llama's back. Llamas, one of the few domesticated animals in the New World, often appear as ceramic effigies. Indigenous to the highlands, they probably carried light loads of goods to the coast, and may also have been domesticated on the coast to some extent. Coastal archaeological excavations have encountered llama remains in burials.

85

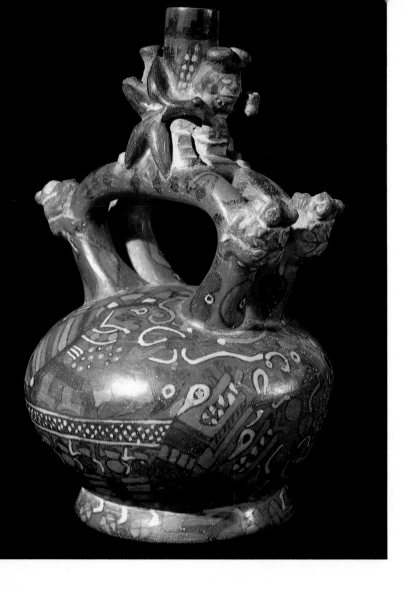

MOCHICA-HUARI CULTURE
Stirrup-spout vessel with deity in boat
Ca. A.D. 700–800
Polychrome ceramic; height 21 cm.
North coast
Amano Museum, Lima

MOCHICA-HUARI CULTURE.   *Stirrup-spout vessel with deity in boat.*

The Tiahuanaco-Huari influence extended to the north coast, where it sometimes blended interestingly with the art of the Mochica, whose power, already waning, was probably completely destroyed by the aggression from the south. This unusual vessel has the basic form of a Mochica globular, stirrup-spout vessel, but the stirrup has been doubled—something unheard of in Mochica times—and appliqués of anthropomorphic birds and men holding plants have been added. The painted design on the bowl—a deity in a reed boat with a snakehead at the bow—is a traditional Mochica design, but the choice of colors and the method of painting with outlined forms come from Tiahuanaco-Huari art.

NASCA-HUARI CULTURE, ATARCO STYLE.   *Double-spout-and-bridge vessel with flying figure.*   *Facing page*

Like the foregoing vessel, this is an excellent example of the accommodation

NASCA-HUARI CULTURE,
ATARCO STYLE
Double-spout-and-bridge vessel with
flying figure
Ca. A.D. 600–700
Polychrome ceramic; height 13 cm.
South coast, Nasca Valley
Amano Museum, Lima

of the highland style to a coastal style. This vessel has a traditional south-coast shape (see pp. 65, 70), but the subject and the geometrized patterning derive from the mountains to the east. The flying anthropomorphic bird is a simplified version of the winged figures from the sides of the Gate of the Sun. Figures on their sides are a convention of the Atarco style, found in one zone of the Nasca Valley. Although similar motifs appear all over the Andes, each locality has its distinctive manner of presenting them.

HUARI CULTURE. *Tapestry tunic.* *p. 88*

This nearly complete Huari tapestry tunic has been placed on a mummy mannequin to simulate the conditions of burial. Huari tunics are usually found like this as the outer surface of a mummy bundle, which contains the wrapped and shrouded deceased inside. In Huari burials the mummy is usually in a seated position, presumably for religious reasons. One of the important pieces of evidence for the existence of extensive Huari influence all over Peru during the Middle Horizon is the fact that burial patterns changed during this period, with the seated position replacing in popularity the older

horizontal one.

This tunic design is composed of a single rectangular design which is repeated with left and right versions and with mirror images of each of these and with color variations. The basic design itself contains a condor head, a puma head, a corn plant, and a human trophy head, all connected by a stepped fret design. The tapestry construction is of the interlocked variety, as is most highland tapestry. The weft is of alpaca. Probably this tunic was made somewhere in the highland centers of the Huari culture but buried on the coast with its highland decedent.

HUARMEY CULTURE. *Tapestry square.*

This alpaca tapestry square is the large decorative neck border of a tunic from the Huarmey culture. To be understood, it should be viewed as folded in half on the diagonal, forming a "V" neck front and back. The remainder of the tunic was undoubtedly of plain cotton. Both the black outlining of the design and the hook pattern came from the Mochica culture far north of the Huarmey Valley. The optical pleasure of the design depends upon the figure/ground reversal of the hook patterns. The technique of construction is slit tapestry with alpaca weft and cotton warp.

HUARMEY CULTURE
Tapestry square
Ca. A.D. 600–900
80 × 79 cm.
Huarmey Valley
Amano Museum, Lima

HUARI CULTURE. *Tapestry tunic.*

This classic Huari tunic has been opened so that both sides may now be seen. The tunic is illustrated here with the opened-up long dimension shown horizontally. This is as each long half was seen in the loom when the weaver was working. However, after completion of the weaving, and joining the two panels, the textile was folded, the sides were sewn up, leaving sleeve openings. It was then turned 90° for use as a tunic.

The apparent pattern complexity is the result of carefully manipulated color variations of a basic repeated pattern. That pattern consists of a rectangular design which is diagonally divided into two images—one is a profile face; the other is a step and wave pattern. This two-part pattern is repeated thousands of times in Huari art, and no doubt had an important symbolic

HUARI CULTURE
Tapestry tunic
Ca. A.D. 800–1000
213×98 cm.
South coast
Amano Museum, Lima

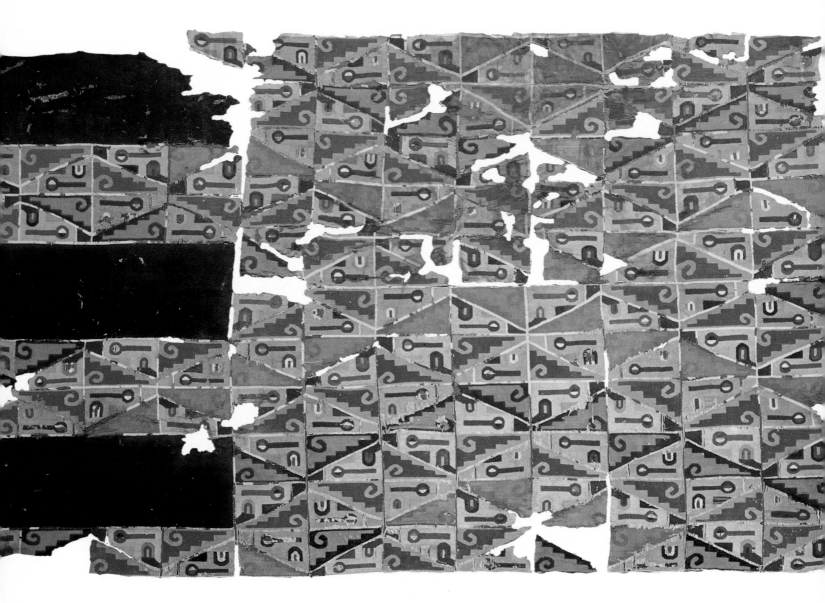

HUARI-DERIVED CULTURE
Mantle with brocading
Ca. A.D. 900
Length 180 cm.
South coast
Amano Museum, Lima

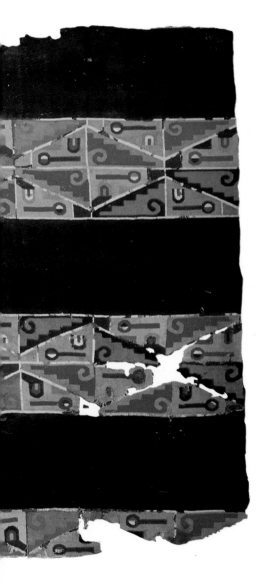

meaning. But each repeat is slightly different. The role of the design may have been comparable to flags in our culture, but in Huari culture every flag was individualized by the artist/weaver. Technically, these tunics are created by interlocked tapestry using alpaca for weft, and using sometimes cotton, sometimes alpaca for warp.

HUARI DERIVED CULTURE. *Mantle with brocading.*

This rectangular mantle, or shoulder cloth of plain weave cotton, has elegant brocaded patterns in each of the four corners. The brightly colored checkerboard pattern, which occurs in two of the corners, is derived from Huari art and simulates Huari tapestry. The repeated profile face has Huari attributes, such as the headdress with puma faces and bird tails, the eye divided into a black half and a white half, and the long tear extending downward from the eye. But of greatest interest is the band which emanates from the mouth suggesting the idea of speech or singing. This profile figure occurs often enough in late Huari art to suggest that a specific reference is being made, perhaps to a speaking deity or to a mythical orator.

The supplemental weft patterning or brocade in the other two corners of the mantle does not in any way come from the textile traditions of Huari, but is a strictly coastal technique. The mantle appears to be the work of a local south coast weaver paying obeisance to the highland art style of Huari. It was probably folded and worn in such a way that the brightly colored corners were displayed.

91

HUARI CULTURE
Four-pointed pile hat
Ca. A.D. 800–1000
16 × 16 × 16 cm.
Palpa, Nasca Valley
Amano Museum, Lima

HUARI CULTURE.   *Four-pointed pile hat.*

Huari graves found in the southern coastal areas of Peru sometimes contain elaborately attired mummies wearing pile hats like this one or wearing head-bands. Both this pile hat tradition and the headband tradition date back to Tiahuanaco, the predecessor culture to Huari. The pile of the hat is of dyed alpaca wool with individual tufts secured during the construction of a knotted cotton base fabric, visible here in worn areas. Huari ceramic and turquoise carved figures are often represented wearing these little square hats, which strike us as appearing pious like a yarmulka or skull cap. The design is of abstracted birds in alternating colors, separated by a row of diamonds. Both motifs are characteristically found on these hats.

TIAHUANACO-HUARI CULTURE.   *Effigy vessel, man with outstretched hands.*   *Facing page*

The poncho, or tunic, depicted on this south-coast vessel has vertical bands of a pattern of odd, repeated faces; this garment is reminiscent of the one on the central figure on the Tiahuanaco Gate of the Sun (p. 79). The clenched fists are hollow and may once have held wooden staffs. The figure wears a

92

Facing page
TIAHUANACO-HUARI CULTURE
Effigy vessel, man with outstretched hands
Ca. A.D. 600–700
Polychrome ceramic; height 29 cm.
South coast
Amano Museum, Lima

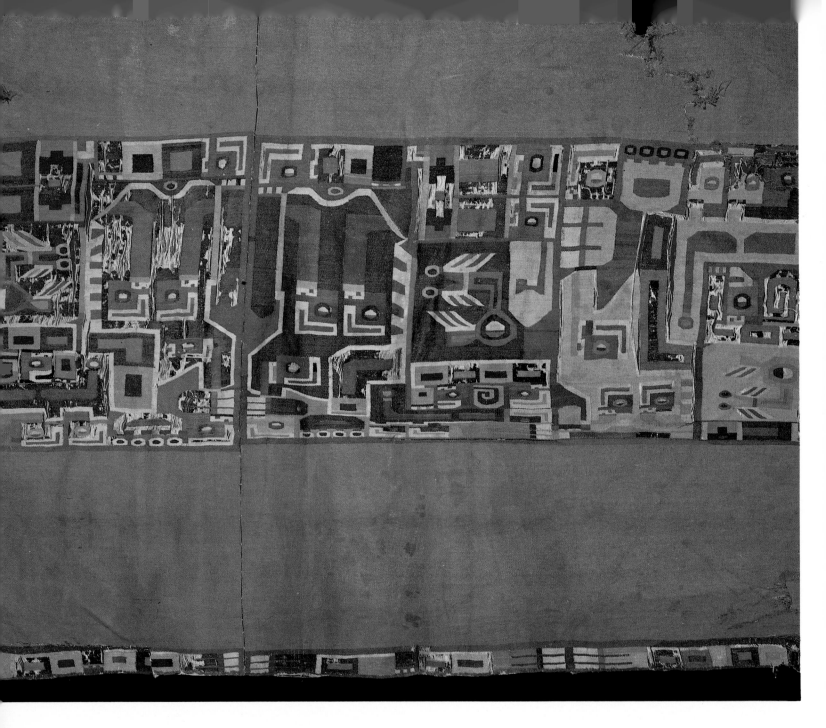

hat with peaked corners, made of pile cloth, or "Peruvian velvet" (see p. 92). A stepped-triangle design decorates its corners and is also seen in the paint of the masklike face. The vessel is almost globular, but the shape has been modified to approximate a human body. Feet are suggested at the base.

HUARI CULTURE. *Tapestry tunic fragments.*

Two panel ends from a Huari tunic have been attached to illustrate the designs of the textile. The full shirt would have been similar to the one shown on page 88. The best preserved of the figures has a green body and is illustrated as a horizontal figure carrying a staff, having a belt flying behind, and an elaborate headdress and wing. The iconography is difficult for us to read

Facing page
HUARI CULTURE
Tapestry tunic fragments
Ca. A.D. 800–1000
52 × 65 cm. (portion illustrated)
Amano Museum, Lima

HUARI CULTURE
Multi-colored tie-dyed mantle
Ca. A.D. 600–1000
57 × 158 cm.
South coast
Amano Museum, Lima

because the design is very condensed at the top. This is because the artist/ weaver actually sat on the long side of the textile while weaving and wove in perspective, with the figure condensed toward the horizon. At the top edge of the illustrated textile, portions of the figure are repeated in very simplified, condensed form. The fine cotton warp, compact alpaca weft and interlock technique make these Huari textile designs seem like paintings.

HUARI CULTURE. *Multi-colored tie-dyed mantle.*

Several extraordinary techniques were combined to produce a brilliant, multicolored effect in this pure alpaca mantle and in similar tunics. First, each of the colored squares was woven separately, then each was tie-dyed. Finally,

95

SOUTH COAST-HUARI CULTURE
Spout-and-strap vessel, fish
Ca. A.D. 600–700
Polychrome ceramic; height 13 cm.
South coast
Amano Museum, Lima

the plain-colored bands were woven in place, having their warps interlocking with those of the colored squares to form a complete textile. It is darning raised to a high art. Such textiles are extremely lightweight although they were made by a weaver for the Huari culture of the high, cold sierra. Their purpose was obviously visual communication and not warmth, almost as if their role was like that of signal flags. If they were warrior outerwear (their rank association is actually unknown), they would have created the world's most colorful infantry.

SOUTH COAST-HUARI CULTURE. *Spout-and-strap vessel, fish.*

Although fish appear on many coastal vessels, effigy fish are relatively rare. This vessel retains the liveliness of the south-coast tradition, but the form of the spout-and-bridge vessel has now been altered; the spout has been lengthened, and the strap is no longer a bridge to a projecting part of the vessel. Here the spout is placed where the dorsal fin might normally be; the ventral fins project at the lower side.

CHIMÚ CULTURE.   *Courtyard and walls at Chanchan.*

The Late Intermediate period, like the Early Intermediate, was marked by a number of regional styles rather than a widespread horizon style.   The Chimú style of the north coast, found generally overlying the old Mochica territory, had as its center the impressive site of Chanchan, which consisted of nine large, high-walled compounds made of adobe bricks.   It is thought that each compound was made for a ruler and closed off when he died and a new ruler began a new compound.   The walls of buildings surrounding expansive courtyards have adobe decoration in designs that look as if they were derived from textiles.   Some walls have an open latticework, presumably to let air flow through.   Ruins of a number of high-walled cities of this period survive.

CHIMÚ CULTURE
Courtyard and walls
Ca. A.D. 900–1476
Adobe
North coast, Chanchan

CHIMÚ CULTURE
Stirrup-spout vessels, musicians
Ca. A.D. 1100–1300
Burnished black ceramic; heights 20–21 cm.
North coast
Amano Museum, Lima

CHIMÚ CULTURE. *Stirrup-spout vessels, musicians.*

Chimú pottery is much like earlier Mochica pottery—the stirrup-spout form remains, as does the convention of placing full-round figures on box-shaped vessels. But the pottery is less various and usually not so finely and creatively made. Most vessels were made in molds; the pottery was, and looks, mass-produced. Effigy figures have stylized faces—there are no portraits in Chimú art. Musical instruments continue to be an important motif. In this group of musicians, the second figure from the right plays reed panpipes. The central figure plays a drum. At either side of this figure, on the same vessel, two small figures play transverse flutes; the figure on the vessel at the left plays the same instrument. This type of flute came into this area after the Mochica era.

CHIMÚ CULTURE. *Stirrup-spout vessel with chili peppers.*

This vessel is garnished with neatly arranged chili peppers, continuing earlier traditions of showing food on pottery. The vessel form might almost be Mochica, except for the little animal that crouches at the base of the spout; this motif—usually a monkey, although here the tail and head suggest that it may be a lizard or iguana—is diagnostic of Chimú ceramics. Whereas most Mochica pottery was bichrome or polychrome, most Chimú vessels are of blackware. Such pottery was burnished and then smoked to give it blackness.

CHIMÚ CULTURE
Stirrup-spout vessel with çhili peppers
Ca. A.D. 1100–1300
Burnished black ceramic; height 24.5 cm.
North coast
Amano Museum, Lima

Facing page
CHIMÚ CULTURE
Double-chambered "whistling" vessel with figures
Ca. A.D. 1300–1476
Burnished black ceramic; height 22 cm.
North coast
Amano Museum, Lima

CHIMÚ CULTURE. *Double-chambered "whistling" vessel with figures.*

p. 101

Double-chambered vessels that acted as whistles are found throughout the Andes, exemplifying a Pre-Columbian love of sound-making objects. Liquid, forcing air through holes in these vessels, caused them to create a sound. This one has a bottle joined to a simplified human body with a full-round head and arms emerging from it. The hands hold what appears to be a root vegetable. The curious head shape, with pulled-out upper corners, is typical of much Chimú pottery. On the bowl of this part of the vessel a figure is depicted in relief, with a knife-shaped headdress and raised hands. The raised-dot background is characteristic of Chimú relief pottery, as is the framing of the scene.

CHIMÚ CULTURE. *Double-chambered "whistling" vessel, woman with child.*

Here a bottle is attached by a bridge to a full-round woman sitting on a square box. She is suckling a child held in a cradle. A hole to emit sound

CHIMÚ CULTURE
Double-chambered "whistling" vessel, woman with child
Ca. A.D. 900–1300
Burnished red ceramic; height 17 cm.
North coast
National Museum of Anthropology and Archaeology, Lima

can be seen in the bridge just behind her head. Both the subject matter and the bottle form are ancient, dating back at least as far as the Chavín era (see pages 20 and 21).

CHIMÚ CULTURE. *Stirrup-spout vessel, men fishing in a reed raft.*

This is an unusually complex and well-made pot, very close to Mochica prototypes (see p. 54). Two men, lying in a reed raft, hold fishing lines. The one on this side of the vessel has hooked a large sting ray, seen in relief on the bowl. On north-coast vessels, designs were often repeated, with slight variations, on the two sides of a globular vessel; therefore, one would expect to find another fish on a line on the other side. With the Chimú, we are in a proto-historical era. At the time of the Spanish conquest, there were still royal legends on the north coast. A legend from the Lambayeque Valley tells of an early king who came there from the south in a reed raft and founded a dynasty.

CHIMÚ CULTURE
Stirrup-spout vessel, men fishing in a reed raft
Ca. A.D. 900–1300
Burnished black ceramic; height 16 cm.
North coast
Amano Museum, Lima

CHIMÚ CULTURE. *Stirrup-spout vessel, two men carrying a mummy bundle.*

Shown here is a simple, hammock-like carrying device, a pole on which a mummy bundle is carried. The swirl motif on the textile was a symbol for "sea" in earlier Mochica art and may indicate here that the dead man has been prepared to go through the sea to the other world. Spanish chroniclers tell us that mummies were periodically taken out and paraded around; such a scene may be shown here. This theme also appears in north-coast art of the later Inca period. The vertical stripes on the headdresses of the carriers may symbolize feathers. The vessel is finely made in a characteristic Chimú shape, with deck figures on a box; the monkey on the spout can just be seen in the background.

CHIMÚ CULTURE. *Open-spout vessel, squash.* *Facing page*

This handsome vessel is formed like a squash with the neck turned back toward the spout so that the shape resembles a seabird with back-turned

CHIMÚ CULTURE
Open-spout vessel, squash
Ca. A.D. 1100–1476
Burnished black ceramic; height 16 cm.
North coast
Amano Museum, Lima

neck. Such punning is common in Andean art. The neck also forms a
handle, although this was probably funerary pottery that was not actually
carried, except perhaps in a burial ritual. Here, the typical Chimú raised-dot
pattern becomes part of the natural texture of the vegetable.

CHIMÚ CULTURE. *Feather tunic.* *p. 106*

This complete feathered tunic, which has been opened up so that both front
and back can be seen, is remarkably complete. The design is bold and perfectly executed, combining abstract representations of fish, pelicans and
waves.
The method of construction (which as a first step attached feathers to
strings), as well as the feathers themselves, probably came from the tropical
forest area just east of the Andes mountains. The technique of feather tunic
construction was very much the same all over ancient Peru, which also suggests that it was an imported one and not of local origin. Feather colors are
naturally very resistant to sun fading, and the colors remain today just as
brilliant as they were on the living bird.

CHIMÚ CULTURE
Feather tunic
Ca. A.D. 1000–1400
86 × 31 cm.
Lambayeque Valley
Amano Museum, Lima

CHANCAY CULTURE. *Chimú tapestry panel with figures and centipedes.*

This tapestry fragment has characteristics which identify it with the Chimú and Mochica cultures of the north of Peru, though it was excavated in the Chancay Valley of central Peru. Such out-of-place finds are sometimes called "trade goods," though we, in this case, have no evidence that the exchange was commercial. It may also suggest that some special site in the Chancay Valley received foreign offerings.

The design consists of square panels which are surrounded by seated figures, reminiscent of the "helper" figures found on Mochica ceramics. Within the panels are frontal figures, each with skirt and headdress, having above and below giant double-headed centipedes. In the later painted textiles from the Chancay Valley, the centipede in the sky becomes arched and resembles a rainbow. The four fragmentary faces in the corners of each panel design are reminiscent of the corner guardian figures in Mochica textiles. The technique is slit tapestry, with alpaca weft and cotton warp.

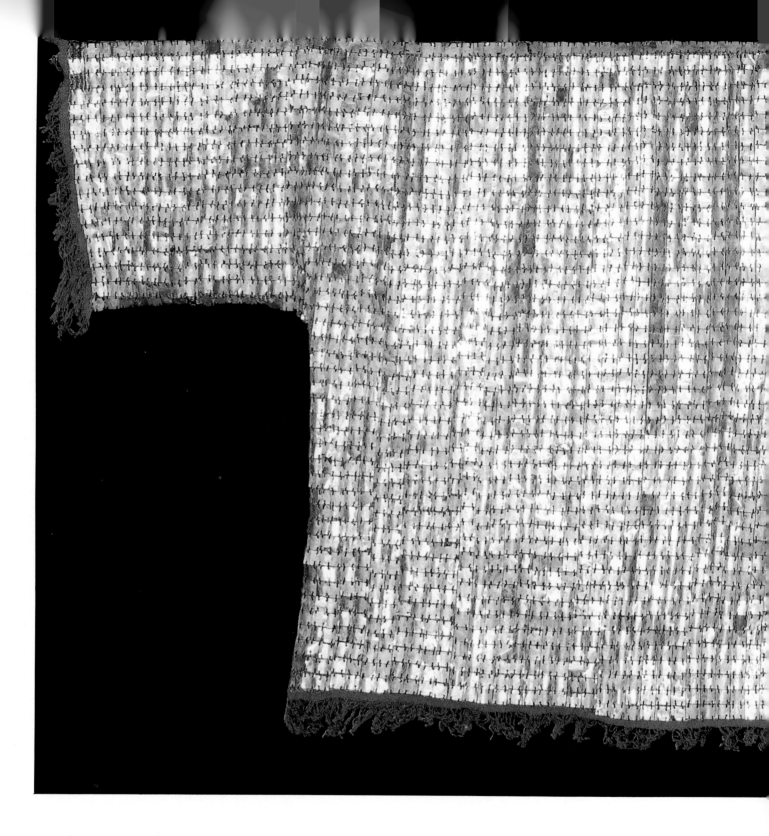

CHIMÚ CULTURE. *Gold appliqued tunic.*

Although this astonishing tunic looks remarkably like a modern disco special, it presumably was the serious attire of an important Chimú leader. Gold seems to have had exactly the same connotations in the Pre-Columbian world as it has in the Western world, and the Chimú kings accumulated vast

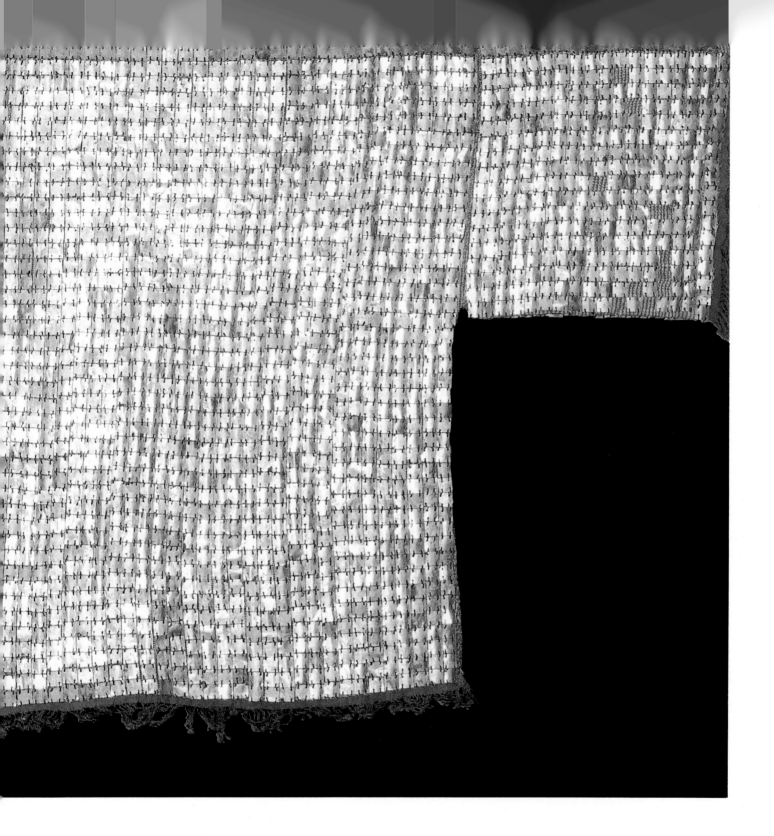

CHIMÚ CULTURE
Gold appliqued tunic
Ca. A.D. 1200–1400
Length 149 cm.
North coast
The Gold Museum, Lima

quantities of it. When the king died, most of his wealth was buried with him, and his burial mound and associated facilities were endowed for perpetual care. These burial mounds were gradually abandoned during Inca times, and have been almost continuously looted since the Spanish conquest. This glittering, golden shirt was probably part of such a royal treasure. Each of the approximately seven thousand golden squares is separately fastened.

CHIMÚ CULTURE. *Stirrup-spout vessel with feline.*

The feline, posed against a raised-dot background, resembles simplified feline sculptures found in the Callejón de Huaylas, in the mountains east of Chimú territory. The feline totally lacks the realism found in earlier Mochica cats. A tiny monkey crouches at the bottom of the spout, and two animal heads, probably those of lizards, are seen on the curving bowl of the vessel. Chimú ceramics imitate or continue earlier traditions; there are no new themes in Chimú iconography. This conservatism is probably in part a simple continuance of tradition and in part a deliberate attempt to identify with the ancestral past.

CHIMÚ CULTURE. *Ceremonial knife, or tumi.* *Facing page*

Chimú goldsmiths hammered large, handsome objects from gold. This knife may have been used for the ritualistic decapitation of a human being or an animal, or it may have been only put into a grave for the use of a chieftain in the other world. The blade is surmounted by a standing

CHIMÚ CULTURE
Stirrup-spout vessel with feline
Ca. A.D. 1100–1300
Burnished black ceramic; height 26 cm.
North coast
Amano Museum, Lima

CHIMÚ CULTURE
Ceremonial knife, or tumi
Ca. A.D. 1100–1300
Hammered sheet gold; height 39.5 cm.
North coast, Lambayeque Valley,
Batán Grande
National Museum of Anthropology and
Archaeology, Lima

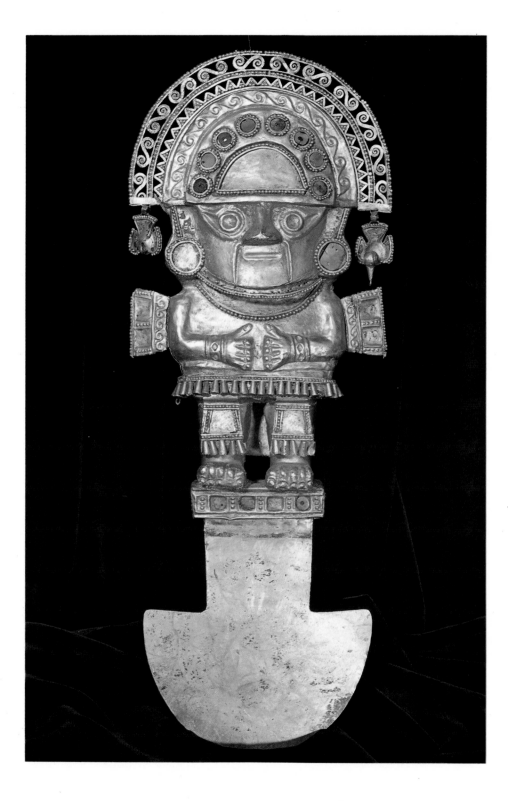

figure with a masklike face—large burial masks made in the Lambayeque
Valley have an almost identical shape. The elaborate deity headdress is
ornamented with granulation, cut and hammered designs, and turquoise or
chrysocolla inlay. At each side of the headdress a hummingbird plunges
downward. One earornament inlay remains. Bells trim the ankles and the
edge of the shirt. There are traces of red cinnabar on the face.

CHIMÚ CULTURE
Double vessel, animal and kero
Ca. A.D. 900–1476
Hammered sheet gold; height 14.5 cm.
North coast
The Gold Museum, Lima

CHIMÚ CULTURE. *Double vessel, animal and* kero,

This vessel was probably sound-making, as most double vessels are (see pp. 101, 102). The shapes of ceramic vessels were imitated in gold for people who were especially powerful, politically and/or spiritually. In this example, a *kero* is attached by a tube to the body of an animal, possibly a dog, who wears a bonnet-like headdress, an unusual feature in Chimú iconography. Under the chin of the animal is the head of a round-eyed creature. Another version of this theme shows that the upper animal is mounting the lower one. The vessel is made of attached pieces of hammered gold. Seams can be seen in the head and neck of the animal and in the body; one can also see where the tube has been soldered to the *kero* with a circular plate.

CHIMÚ CULTURE. *Beaker, or* kero, *with staff-bearing deity.* *Facing page*

Beakers like this one, of thick, heavy gold, are found with a variety of designs; they have sometimes been found in sets, like an elegant dinner service. Relatively few gold artifacts have been discovered archaeologically in Peru. Most of the gold that was above ground at the time of the conquest was melted down by the Spanish conquerors. Much, however, had been put in burials or caches, and has been found largely by grave-robbers. The staff-bearing figure here is reminiscent of earlier examples in Chavín and Tiahuanaco art, but the hemispherical headdress is characteristic of the north coast. The figure is framed in a band of the stepped-triangle-and-swirl motif.

CHIMÚ CULTURE
Beaker, or kero, *with staff-bearing deity*
Ca. A.D. 1100–1300
Hammered sheet gold; height 21 cm.
North coast, Lambayeque Valley, Batán Grande (?)
National Museum of Anthropology and Archaeology, Lima

CHIMÚ CULTURE. *Ear ornament with seabird.*

Ear ornaments were widely worn in Pre-Columbian America by important people—mostly men—and gods. (Great chieftains were thought of—or thought of themselves—as gods.) A perforation was made in the earlobe for the insertion of a tube, like this, or another form of ornament. When the Spanish conquerors came to Peru and saw the chiefly earlobes pulled down by the weight of rich ornaments, they nicknamed the chieftains *orejones*, "big ears." This disk, framed with small beads, features a seabird with a fish dangling from its mouth. Danglers were often attached to gold objects by loops so that they could hang freely and reflect glittering light (see pp. 57, 111).

CHIMÚ CULTURE
Ear ornament with seabird
Ca. A.D. 900–1476
Hammered and cut sheet gold;
diameter 12 cm.
North coast
National Museum of Anthropology and
Archaeology, Lima

CHIMÚ CULTURE. *Staff-cup.*

This unusual and elaborate object made in three separate parts, with a cup at the top, could be grasped like a staff, so that a priest or chieftain might imitate a staff god (see p. 113). The cut-out, incised, and hammered central portion has large mythic monsters, small human figures, birds, and fish. The cup and base are also worked with designs. Such an object is evidence of the complex religious and ceremonial life of these people, and of the skill of their goldsmiths. It is reported that when the Inca captured the Chimú capital, whence this object is reported to come, they took the goldsmiths to Cuzco, and that Chimú gold objects were also removed to the Inca capital, where they were reworked for Inca purposes.

CHIMÚ CULTURE
Staff-cup
Ca. A.D. 900–1476
Hammered and cut gold; height 38 cm.
North coast, Moche Valley, Chanchan
National Museum of Anthropology and
Archaeology, Lima

115

CHIMÚ CULTURE. *Staff-cup.*

Gourds have probably been used as utensils as long as there have been people in Peru. Modern pyroengraved gourds are bought by tourists as souvenirs; they are also used by country people today. Because of the dry preservation conditions on the coast, a few ancient gourds remain. This one, with complex engraved designs, is set with extraordinary elaboration. It rests on a wooden jaguar, inlaid with shell, which, in turn, stands on an inlaid pedestal. The complex form is reminiscent of the gold staff-cup on p. 115.

CHIMÚ CULTURE
Staff-cup
Ca. A.D. 900–1476
Pyroengraved gourd and wood inlaid with shell; height 39.5 cm.
North coast
Rafael Larco Herrera Museum, Lima

CHANCAY CULTURE. *Litter end.*

Another regional kingdom of the Late Intermediate period with a distinct art style is named for a town on the central coast, a little north of Lima. In Andean art, figures are usually scaled according to their importance, not to suggest perspective. The contrast in figure size seen here probably indicates that the large figures are supernatural beings. They wear feather headdresses and hold staffs—the artist has not made the fingers grip the shaft, but has simply put the staff adjacent to the hand. A central staff stands between two smaller figures, one of whom is held by the hair by the large figure at left, and the other by the hand by the other large figure. The framing border of birds is reminiscent of textiles of this period. Important people and supernatural beings are shown litter-borne. The dead were also carried in litters.

CHANCAY CULTURE
Litter end
Ca. A.D. 1100–1476
Wood with paint and shell inlay;
height 75 cm.
Central coast, Pisquillo Chico (?)
Amano Museum, Lima

117

CHANCAY CULTURE.   *Open-spout vessel, pot-carrier.*

Chancay ceramics are unmistakable dull-finished, open-spout effigy vessels like large, pale dolls.   This one takes the form of a man carrying on his back pots held by ropes across the shoulders.   Discs, which look at first like ear ornaments, are counterweights for the load.   The dark panel beneath each eye can probably be traced back to a Chavín motif, but the jowliness of the face is reminiscent of the Middle Horizon vessel on p. 93.   A variation of the stepped-triangle-and-swirl motif decorates the belt and cuffs.   Most of these vessels are not flat-bottomed and cannot stand on their own; they were apparently made to be stood up in the desert sand.

CHANCAY CULTURE
Open-spout vessel, pot-carrier
Ca. A.D. 1100–1476
Ceramic with gray and white; height 52 cm.
Central coast
Amano Museum, Lima

CHANCAY CULTURE. *Open-spout vessel, man with feline.*

Chancay vessels are usually made in the form of ovoid human figures. This man, with protruding eyeballs, fat cheeks and tiny mouth, may have been suffering from a disfiguring illness. He has unusual face paint, which is repeated on his right hand. The hands are made of straps of clay like suspension devices. On his left shoulder, a tiny spotted feline is attached by a spotted string to the left hand. This may be a jaguar cub or a smaller feline, a margay or an ocelot. The figure has one pendant-disk ear ornament, suspended from a hole in the ear; there is no trace of an ornament in the other ear. This is most unusual, for, although some may now be missing, ear ornaments were always worn in pairs. The jagged line at the waist is reminiscent of that seen on an earlier Mochica deity (see p. 49). The feet protrude on the lower part of the vessel. Earlier ovoid or globular vessels would have shown feet at the bottom, if at all. In Chancay art, the vessel is no longer a synonym for a human body.

CHANCAY CULTURE
Open-spout vessel, man with feline
Ca. A.D. 1100–1476
Orange ceramic with gray; height 29 cm.
Central coast
Amano Museum, Lima

CHANCAY CULTURE
Open-spout vessel, seabird
Ca. A.D. 1100–1476
Ceramic; height 40 cm.
Central coast
Amano Museum, Lima

CHANCAY CULTURE.   *Open-spout vessel, seabird.*

This bird effigy vessel takes the same ovoid form as the human Chancay
figures, but the spout is placed at the back of the neck rather than at the top
of the head, and the bird head curving forward makes the form more graceful,
even though it is less elaborate than similar forms from other cultures.

CHANCAY CULTURE. *Standing figure with raised arms.*

This figure wears what looks like a prototypical sweatsuit. Clothing is usually not well-defined in Chancay art, and the depiction of trousers is extremely rare anywhere in Pre-Columbian America. The raised hands further suggest someone doing exercises, but this is a typical pose for Chancay figures. Again, the face has painted designs and looks disfigured by disease. It is broad; the eyes are round and prominent. This figure, like the one on p. 118, has counterweights on the shoulders.

CHANCAY CULTURE
Standing figure with raised arms
Ca. A.D. 1100–1476
Ceramic with white and gray; height 58 cm.
Central coast
Amano Museum, Lima

CHANCAY CULTURE
Chancay house of dolls
Ca. A.D. 1200–1400
29×45×27 cm.
Chancay Valley
Amano Museum, Lima

CHANCAY CULTURE.   *Chancay house of dolls.*

One of the most charming textile constructions to come from the Chancay culture is this beautifully preserved house model with its eight richly colored dolls.   Two central figures at the rear appear to be male and female, and the figure on the right holds a cup, suggesting the libations at a marriage ceremony.   Both the facial painting of the figures and the patterning of the outside of the house provide a representation of Chancay Valley life, giving color and vitality to our images of this vibrant and productive central coast Pre-Columbian culture.   One of the figures at the rear wears a bird-patterned tapestry tunic, and several have gauze shawls, all closely resembling actual recovered textiles.

CHANCAY CULTURE. *Tapestry doll faces.*

Most cultures of the world produce painted or carved doll faces, but the weaving oriented Chancay culture of Peru produced these custom woven faces for dolls. The facial pattern suggests that facial painting is being represented, and there is some evidence to suggest that this particular zig-zag pattern is found only on female faces. The textile construction is of slit tapestry with alpaca weft and cotton warp and it was made on a miniature back strap loom.

CHANCAY CULTURE
Tapestry doll faces
Ca. A.D. 1200–1400
Amano Museum, Lima

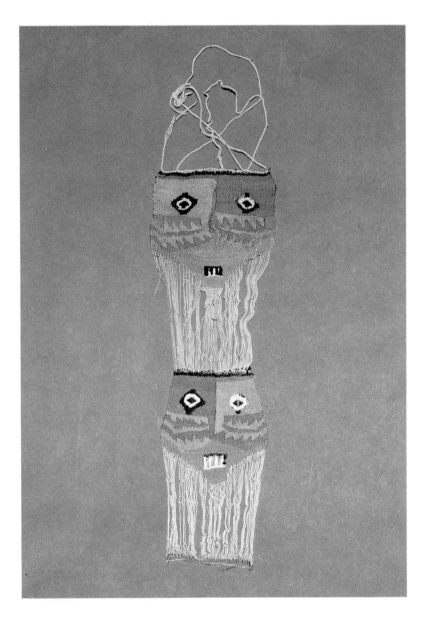

CHIMÚ CULTURE
Tasseled red tunic
Ca. A.D. 1200–1400
58 × 162 cm.
Chancay Valley
Amano Museum, Lima

CHIMÚ CULTURE. *Tasseled red tunic.*

This highly decorated tunic actually came from the Chancay Valley, although its characteristics are typical of what we know of late Chimú fancy tunics. The tunic demonstrates the close relationship which existed between these two culture areas. It is tapestry construction with intermittent structural wefts and with supplemental tassels and textile discs. The weaving method for the discs remains a mystery, though they apparently have spiral warp and radial weft. The variety of techniques and the brilliant red dye make this one of the most extravagant textiles known from the Chancay Valley, and it is one of only a few such tunics in existence. Whether its use was religious or secular, or both, we do not know, but it is clear that the purpose was to overwhelm the viewer, a task which it continues to fulfill to this day.

TIAHUANACO-HUARI CULTURE
Spearthrower, detail

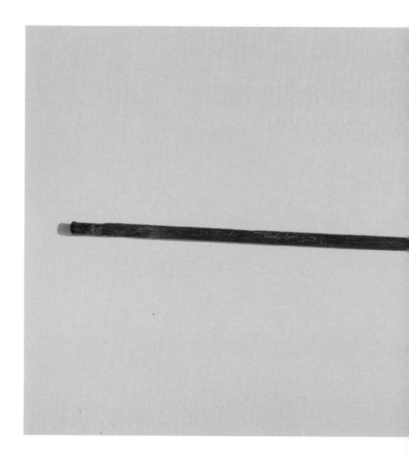

TIAHUANACO-HUARI CULTURE. *Spearthrower and detail.*

Throughout the New World, the spearthrower—an artificial extension of the human arm (the longer the arm, the greater the throwing distance)—was the common weapon. The bow and arrow were used by tribes in the Amazon Basin, but the more civilized people of the highlands and the coast used the spearthrower. Clubs were used in close battle. This is a Middle Horizon example from the south coast, but similar weapons were used over a long period of time in the Andes. Figures are carved on the handle and the thumb rest. The detail shows the two figures carved on the end. Putting one figure on top of another is not common in the art of Peru; in this case, the idea seems to have been suggested by the long, thin form of the weapon.

TIAHUANACO-HUARI CULTURE
Spearthrower
Ca. A.D. 500–900
Wood; length 67 cm.
South coast
National Museum of Anthropology and
Archaeology, Lima

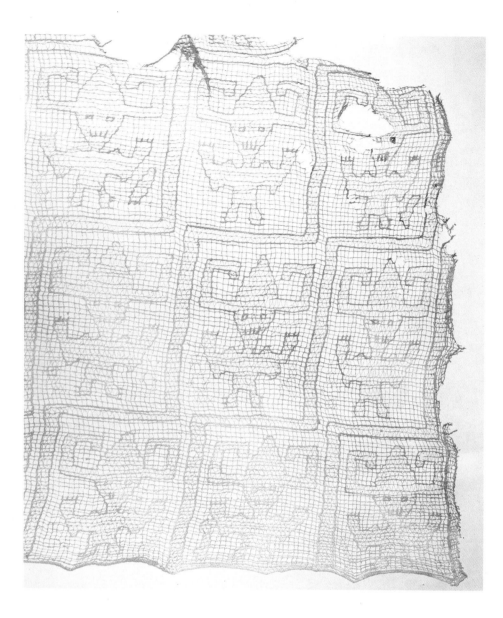

CHANCAY CULTURE. *Open fabric with anthropomorphic design.*

This light-weight, delicate, resilient fabric merits admiration and study. Whether used as shawl or head covering, it seems certain that witchcraft was involved and that it might well be called a "witching veil." It is made entirely of fine, crepe-spun, single strand, cotton yarn; part is spun in one direction, and that used for the eyes and figure outline, spun with the opposite twist. In parts of Peru, yarn twisted counter to the spinner's normal practice is believed to give it some magical quality. Such yarns are today used in witchcraft, for protection and good luck.

The loom-made base fabric has spaced warps and wefts, the intersections held by knots creating squares bounded by pairs of yarns. Over this, the

128

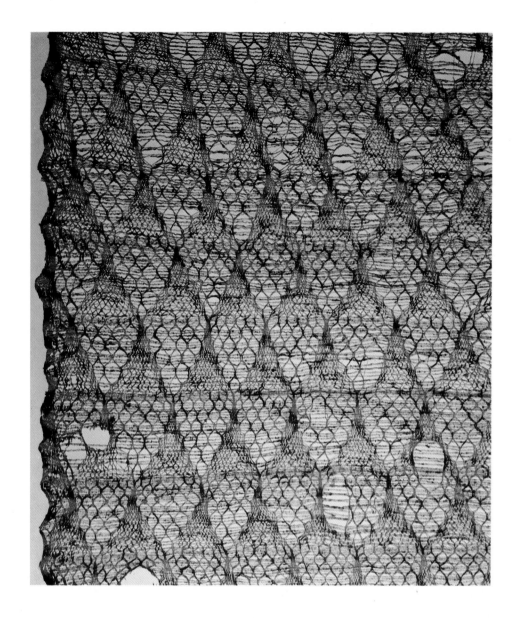

magical yarn is embroidered to create the eyes and outlines. Where areas are filled in loosely with a single strand, the twist of the yarn matches the base fabric yarns.

CHANCAY CULTURE. *Gauze with triangular patterning.*

This brown cotton gauze has been structurally designed during the weaving process by manipulating the warps, creating patterns of alternating gauze weave. The wefts are spaced regularly throughout the whole design. After the weaving was completed, the textile was pattern dyed with a resist technique—probably tie dye.

CHANCAY CULTURE. *Open fabric with tapestry-like design*.

This gauze weave has a design produced by extra-weft interlacing using two different colors. The design consists of pelican-like bird profiles, a frequent figure in Chancay textiles, and a reasonable one, since the center of the Chancay culture was very close to the Pacific shore. The textile is entirely of cotton.

CHANCAY CULTURE. *Resist-patterned plain weave*.

Facing page

A fragment of lightweight cotton plain weave has been patterned with a three-color resist design. This design, which has alternating colors within the

CHANCAY CULTURE
Open fabric with tapestry-like design
Ca. A.D. 1200–1400
40 × 28 cm.
Chancay Valley
Amano Museum, Lima

CHANCAY CULTURE
Resist-patterned plain weave
Ca. A.D. 1200–1400
85 × 103 cm. (size of entire piece)
Chancay Valley
Amano Museum, Lima

CHANCAY CULTURE
Open fabric with fish design
Ca. A.D. 1200–1400
69 × 98 cm.
Chancay Valley
Amano Museum, Lima

checkerboard, is so abstracted that its representational meaning is lost, though it resembles the richly patterned Moche Valley wall murals. Repeat patterning occurs more frequently toward the end of Pre-Colombian times in ancient Peru. The plain weave material seems almost identical to modern cotton cloth, but the techniques of painting and patterning such thin material are not fully understood.

CHANCAY CULTURE. *Open fabric with fish design.* p. 131

Another example of the delicate construction used in the example shown on page 128 and explained in the caption with it. The motif suggests the big-eyed, flat-bodied fish, perhaps stingrays, with which the people of the coastal Chancay culture were, no doubt, intimately familiar. Such fabrics seem to be restricted to the Chancay area.

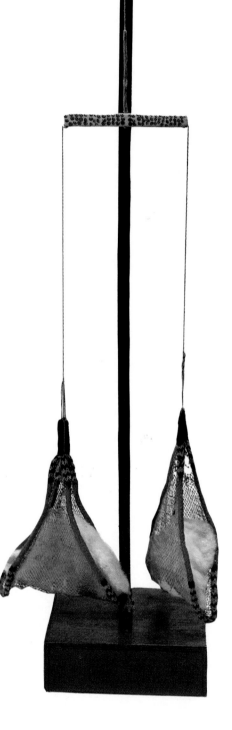

CHANCAY CULTURE
Balance scale with nets
Ca. A.D. 1200–1400
39 × 11 cm.
Chancay Valley
Amano Museum, Lima

CHANCAY CULTURE. *Balance scale with nets.*

This balancing scale is constructed entirely of textiles and wood. Conceptually it is exactly like the balancing scales of European culture, which however would have been made of metal. The difference is instructive. Ancient Peru was a textile-oriented culture; so much so, in fact, that it would be entirely appropriate to refer in a broad way to the whole time period of the high cultures of ancient Peru as the Textile Age, in the same sense that one refers to the Stone Age or the Bronze Age. Textile construction was the primary technology of the Pre-Colombian world, and new textile techniques spread quickly through the cultures of Peru. Technical analysis is therefore of great assistance in the chronological placement of textiles.

In Peru, in addition to clothing, much of the material culture was related to textile production. Suspension bridges were in a sense textile structures. House walls were often of will matting. The balance scale nets illustrated here are but one of the wide range of minor technological objects which were essentially textile creations. The Chancay practice of burying with the deceased the artifacts associated with daily life has provided us with an extensive picture of the objects in use in that vigorous Late Intermediate Period culture.

CHANCAY CULTURE. *Back-strap loom.* *Facing page*

Chancay looms with unfinished weaving are often found accompanying the deceased, but they normally have white cotton warp and weft faced weaving. This loom is an unusual type in that the weaving, which is in the process of being accomplished, is warp faced, using red alpaca warps. However, half of the warps have disintegrated and disappeared, no doubt because they were of a different color whose dye was ultimately destructive to the fiber. The wooden implement inserted in the warps is called a sword and is used for compacting the wefts. The heddle, which is used in separating the warps for insertion of the wefts, is also extant in the loom.

Although there is no archaeological evidence that textiles were ever used as wall hanging in the Pre-Colombian world of Peru, the size and technical characteristics of certain pieces strongly suggest that possibility. This enormous tapestry, with little paired figures all facing the same way, suggests that its use may have been as a wall hanging, but does not actually rule out use as a shoulder shawl or mantle. The alternating squares of the paired figures and of the doubled geometric pattern suggest some kind of interlocking meaning. The top and bottom borders have cats and birds, interacting natural enemies, then as now.

The tapestry of alpaca weft and cotton warp was woven in ten separate matched panels, in slit tapestry technique, and implies a well-organized group effort, rather than individual artistic genius.

CHANCAY CULTURE
Back-strap loom
Ca. A.D. 1200–1400
91 × 39 × 14 cm.
Huacan—Huacho
Amano Museum, Lima

CHANCAY CULTURE. *Slit tapestry tunic.*

This beautifully structured slit tapestry tunic looks as if it had been designed by an architect—a perfect matrix of 16 squares on each side of the tunic front. The matrix frame contains a repeated pattern of fish, aligned as if they were swimming through channels. Within the frames, though, are stately birds, obviously the dominant theme of the tunic. The birds hold something in their beaks which cannot be identified. Beneath is a row of lively cats, completing the Chancay triumvirate of animals from the three worlds of air, earth and water. Finally, at the bottom, is a row of feathers simulated in tapestry. Each of the feathers has a color gradation from stem to tip, just as real feathers often do. The textile is constructed in slit tapestry technique, using alpaca for weft and cotton for warp.

CHANCAY CULTURE. *Tapestry coca bag.* *p. 136*

Coca bags have been a normal part of the wearing apparel of the native Peruvian male from the Early Horizon to today. The bags, suspended by straps from the shoulder, are used for carrying coca leaves, which are chewed with lime as a mild stimulant. The design of the coca bag is an important male status symbol today, and no doubt always was. Very early coca bags had suspended from them miniature representations of human trophy heads, and tassels such as those attached to this coca bag are no doubt derived from that tradition. The face and its associated wave geometry may also be related to that trophy head tradition.

The colors of pink and yellow are traditional ones for Chancay. Construction is slit tapestry with alpaca weft and cotton warp.

CHANCAY AND HUARMEY CULTURES. *Boxes and a basket.* *Facing page*

The weaver's basket in the top illustration has been constructed by oblique interlacing of reeds into the rectangular box-with-lid form. The balls of cotton thread and the weaving shuttle inside are, no doubt, ones used by the Pre-Colombian weaver with whom this basket was buried. Very little Pre-Colombian basketry has been preserved, and examples such as this indicate something of the workmanship and materials which were probably characteristic. The basket is probably from the Chancay Valley.

The carved box in the center illustration is probably also from the Chancay Valley. The design consists of wave patterns, step patterns, and figures with elaborate headdresses. The designs are reminiscent of the stucco art found on the walls of Chanchan, the Chimú capital, a city whose style was highly influential in the Chancay Valley far to its south.

The box at the bottom illustrates still another box-making technique. Canes have been used both to form the outer frame of the box and to form the side panels. The canes have been wrapped with colored threads both to form the design and to hold the canes together. The technique is one which came from the Mochica heartland, but the actual design on the box is of a three-

CHANCAY CULTURE
Tapestry coca bag
Ca. A.D. 1200–1400
18 × 15 cm.
Chancay Valley
Amano Museum, Lima

136

CHANCAY AND HUARMEY CULTURES
Boxes and a basket
Ca. A.D. 1000–1500
Amano Museum, Lima

137

tailed bird typical of those found on Huarmey textiles. Undoubtedly, this also is a weaver's box, found in the tomb of the owner, and is probably from the Huarmey Valley.

CHANCAY CULTURE. *Bird tapestry panel.*

This panel of slit tapestry with animal figures is one of the most characteristic works produced for the grave goods of the Chancay Valley. Its pink background is the dominant color of all Chancay textiles, and the yellows, tans, blacks and whites are the normal secondary ones. The repeated patterning, with only slight color variation and with no formal variation, is also characteristic. In earlier centuries Peruvian weavers of most cultures had

138

CHANCAY CULTURE
Bird tapestry panel
Ca. A.D. 1200–1400
70 × 107 cm.
Amano Museum, Lima

much greater coloristic and formal variation in repeated pattern work, the exception being the Mochica culture of the north.

The pattern here represents, as dominant, the strutting bird with a royal headdress, holding a frog in his beak. Beneath is a row of monkeys holding staffs—normally symbols of authority in Peruvian art. Technically, the construction is of slit tapestry with alpaca wefts and cotton warps.

CHANCAY CULTURE. *Belt with tassels.*

This large and elaborate tapestry band with medallions and tassels was presumably worn as a belt with a ritual costume. The designs of the belt proper are mostly Mochica in origin, as are most of the designs found on Chancay textiles, but the lozenge-shaped diamond designs seem to represent feathers in a fashion very similar to later Inca designs. Perhaps the Incas picked up the design from this coastal culture which they conquered. The fringed medallions at the end of the belt show a human figure with a double-headed snake around his neck. Attached to the medallions are fringed faces which undoubtedly represent human trophy heads—not exactly a festive note to our eyes, but suggestive of the seriousness of all the imagery on the belt. The belt is constructed of slit tapestry with cotton warps and alpaca wefts, with fringe and decorative parts also of alpaca.

CHANCAY CULTURE
Belt with tassels
Ca. A.D. 1200–1400
477 × 10 cm.
Amano Museum, Lima

139

CHANCAY CULTURE. *Face-patterned double-cloth.*

Facing page

This panel of repeat patterned double cloth was constructed with two complete sets of warp and weft, one brown set and one white set. The two layers are woven simultaneously and interpenetrate to form the pattern, which has a color reverse on the other side. The pattern itself is an abstract two-eyed fish face with the background and the figure of identical form, so that optical figure/ground reversal occurs.

The earliest recorded interlocking patterns of this type are from the textiles of the Gallinazo culture of the North coast, and are a thousand years older than this Chancay textile.

CHANCAY CULTURE. *Rectangular-patterned double-cloth.*

The grid with infill pictures is a common format for Chancay art, and in this exquisite fragment of double-cloth the familiar form becomes a classic. The grid frame itself is patterned with little men who surround, but are secondary to, the animal figures which are thereby given almost dinosaur-like scale. The animal figures consist of those mortal enemies—birds and cats. The birds are long-necked coastal birds and each holds a fish in its beak. The cats are big-eyed and each holds a staff. The dominance of animals and animal deities in Chancay art clearly suggests an animistic religion for the culture. Technically, the fragment is constructed of brown and white double-cloth, with the colors reversed on the opposite side.

141

COASTAL CULTURE. *Figure in headdress and loincloth.*

Wooden figures of various kinds were carved all along the coast for centuries. Some appear on the ends of implements (see p. 143); others were carved simply as figures. Some have been found as grave markers; others were deeply buried in the guano of seabirds on islands off the coast. Many of the island-found ones are in the form of prisoners or sacrificial victims with bound wrists; they probably represent offerings to the fertility of the sea. This figure seems to be making a gesture of obeisance or surrender. Wooden objects comprise one of the few kinds of coastal sculpture. Both stone and

Facing page
ICA CULTURE
Tomb post in form of an agricultural implement, and detail
A.D. 1476–1534
Wood; height 2.27 m.
South coast, Ica Valley
National Museum of Anthropology and Archaeology, Lima

COASTAL CULTURE
Figure in headdress and loincloth
Ca. A.D. 1100–1476
Wood; height 86 cm.
Amano Museum, Lima

wood were scarce on the coast—few trees grow in the arid conditions—but, since wood is more easily transportable, there are more wooden sculptures than stone ones. Wooden sculpture must have been transported over long distances, probably in reed rafts, for figures of north-coast style have been found on south-coast islands.

ICA CULTURE.   *Tomb post in form of an agricultural implement.*

Several of these artifacts were found by archaeologists in a Late Horizon burial. They were placed upright, and sheathed with gold and silver and red resin paint. Never used as tools, they were enlarged and elaborated versions of digging boards. Andean chieftains took responsibility for the agricultural fertility of their people, on both practical and supernatural levels, so these are appropriate symbolic grave objects. A number of these posts, or boards, are known, with varying numbers of figures on the top. This has five figures, holding hands. Below them is a textile-inspired band of birds surmounted by a stepped triangle, and, below this, a fountain-like variation on the stepped-triangle-and-swirl motif. A fretted bird design is repeated down the side of the handle; at the top of the blade stand four figures with hemispherical headdresses.

CHANCAY CULTURE. *Sleeved tunic.*

This boldly designed sleeved tunic uses alternating colors to create a form of figure/ground reversal art. The iconography consists of a wave pattern, which might represent the ocean, a step pattern, which might represent the mountains, and double-headed mythical birds. These three elements are frequently found in Chancay art and suggest the possibility that land, sea and air were aspects of the Chancay weavers' cosmos.

The weaving is slit tapestry using dyed alpaca wefts and cotton warps. The color variations within solid color areas are created by slightly differing weft dye lots, which seem to be a very purposeful part of the artist/weaver's conception. One sleeve is now missing. The proportions of the tunic are such that perhaps it should be referred to as a "shoulder tunic."

CHANCAY CULTURE
Sleeved tunic
Ca. A.D. 1200–1400
45×55 cm.
Chancay Valley
Amano Museum, Lima

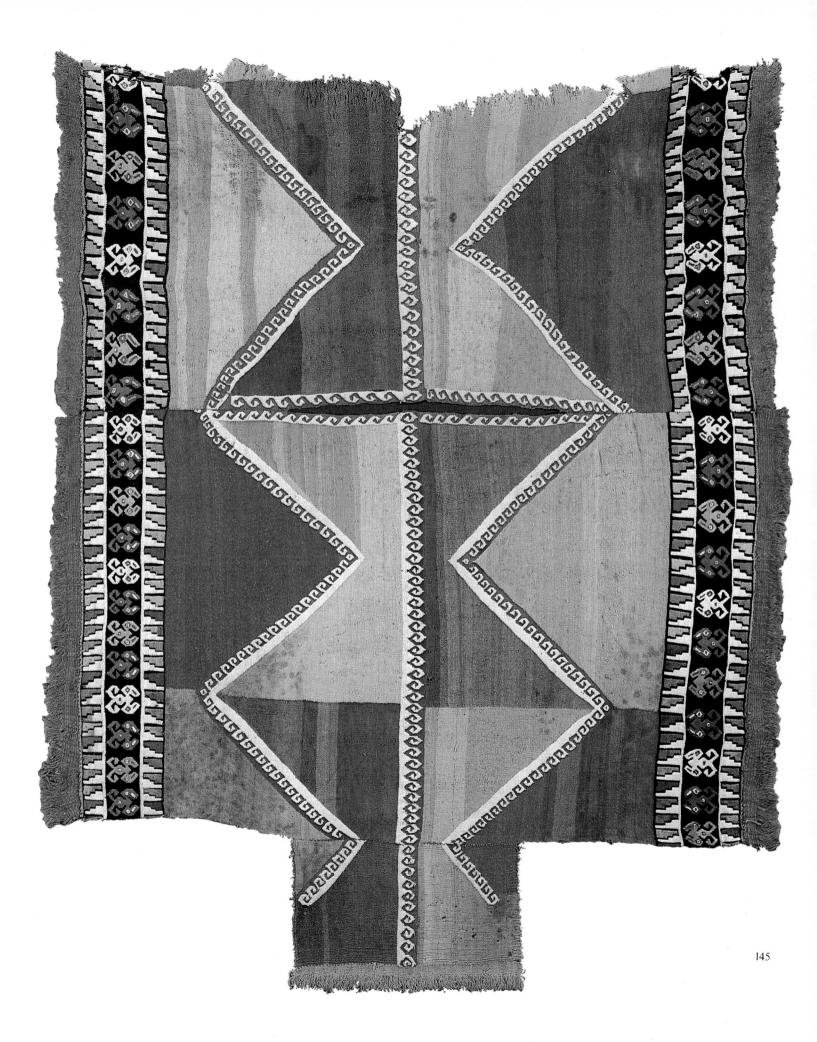

CHIMÚ CULTURE. *Tapestry tunic with golden spangles.*

It may seen unnecessary to our eyes to have added the gold to this tawny-toned tapestry tunic, such is the charm of the tapestry design itself, but perhaps the gold carries status which no textile design could equal. The representation is a row of trees with monkeys in the limbs above plucking

CHIMÚ CULTURE
Tapestry tunic with golden spangles
Ca. A.D. 1200
50.9 × 118 cm.
Los Angeles County Museum

fruit for the aide below who holds the bag. This lighthearted genre scene hardly seems compatible with the weight and seriousness of the gold with which it is underlined. The figures at the bottom row are probably cats. The technique of the textile is slit tapestry with alpaca weft and cotton warp, with the golden-toned autumn colors which are characteristic of the fabrics from the north coast of Peru.

147

INCA CULTURE
Stirrup-spout vessel, two parrots
A.D. 1476–1534
Ceramic with white slip and red and black paint; height 17 cm.
North coast
Amano Museum, Lima

INCA CULTURE. *Stirrup-spout vessel, two parrots.*

The ware and the rim added to the spout tell us that this is a Late Horizon vessel, although it is a traditional north-coast subject. The little animal at the base of the spout on Chimú pots has been reduced to a round blob of clay with an indentation. Parrots, indigenous to the Amazon Basin, often appear in coastal art, frequently in pairs (see also p. 72). The fact that coastal artists knew so well what the creatures of the Amazon Basin looked like indicates considerable traffic across the mountains. This had probably been true for millennia, but it was especially so with the system of Inca roads. Two great north-south roads united the empire, one along the coast, the other in the highlands; there were also east-west roads.

ICA CULTURE. *Jar with geometric designs.* *Facing page*

This elegant and precise form was made with coils of clay, not with a wheel. It has textile-like, zoned decoration, including a step-fret design and a band of triangles that probably derive from the head of a snake or a sting ray. Such abstract decoration is characteristic of late pre-Hispanic art in the

ICA CULTURE
Jar with geometric designs
Ca. A.D. 1300–1476
Polychrome ceramic, white and black on red; height 24 cm.
South coast
Amano Museum

Andes. The essences of the fish, birds, plants, and gods that appeared in earlier south-coast art are here reduced to symbolic patterns. Like the Chancay vessels, the base of this one is not flat. It is now supported by a modern ring; in the past, it would have been stood up in sand. This type of pottery was traded widely; it has been found on the central coast and up in the highlands.

ICA-CHINCHA CULTURE. *Feathered tunic.*

Feather work accomplished the most brilliant color patterning of all forms of clothing construction. To the Andean cultures of both the coastal deserts and the cold sierra, the importation of tropical bird feathers from jungle areas must have been a most remarkable luxury. The feathers were first fastened by their quills in rows to the cotton strings. Then these patterned rows were sewn to a cotton backing cloth or tunic.

The style of designs on feather work does not relate closely to the style of designs on other artifacts, and so it is difficult to identify feather work. The figures represented here, for example, are not found on Ica textiles or ce-

ICA-CHINCHA CULTURE
Feathered tunic
Ca. A.D. 1200–1400
90 × 51.5 cm. (complete panel)
Ica Valley
Amano Museum, Lima

ramics. Stick figures like these are, however, found as hillside line drawings far south of Ica, and also as glyphic stone carvings. The facial feathers and certain other feathers appear to have been somewhat reworked and restored, so that it is difficult to be certain about the characteristics of the original facial designs.

CHANCAY CULTURE. *Pattern samplers.*

Three samplers have been sewn together, probably in ancient times, to form this marvelously complex textile mosaic. The designs are almost entirely concerned with birds, and in some cases individual species could be identified. Some special connection between birds and weaving may be implied. Perhaps there was a weaving deity with avian characteristics. In one of the designs, two running figures occur, each carrying a spindle of thread and each having a bird tail and feather headdress. In another, a pair of birds clasps a weaving implement. In addition to the design samples, however, various weaving techniques are tried out, including slit tapestry, complementary weft patterning, and warp manipulation. The colors, predominantly pink with yellows and tans as well as black and white, are characteristic of the slit tapestry work from this late culture of the Chancay Valley.

CHANCAY CULTURE
Pattern samplers
Ca. A.D. 1200–1400
80 × 43 cm.
Huara, Chancay Valley
Amano Museum, Lima

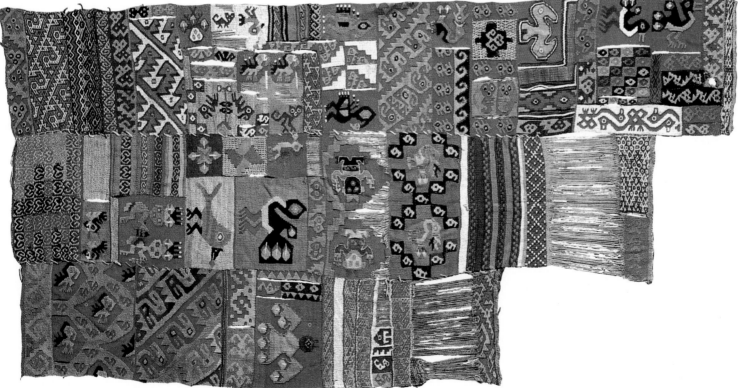

V   Late Horizon Period

A.D. 1476—1534

INCA CULTURE.   Intihuatana, *"hitching post of the sun,"*
Machu Picchu.

Machu Picchu is an outpost hidden on a steep hill surrounded by higher hills above a sharp curve of the Urubamba River.   Strategically placed so that one can see down into the river valley on both sides, the site guards a pass to the Amazon Basin.   It must also have had a long history as a sacred place. This picture shows the Inca fascination with stone.   They had legends of men who were turned to stones and stones that became men.   Their fine, mortarless masonry is world-famous.   They sometimes left rock in natural formations, and sometimes modified natural outcroppings in to non-geometrical shapes, as if imitating nature.   In the center of this picture is the famous stone where, legend tells us, the sun was "tied" on the winter solstice. Such an instrument, which looks like sculpture, was placed in all cities to measure the sun shadow.   Its usage is not completely understood, but it worked more or less like a sun dial.   This is the only one that survives.

INCA CULTURE
Intihuatana, *"hitching post of the sun"*
A.D. 1476–1534
Southern highlands, Machu Picchu

INCA CULTURE. *Female figure.*

Figures like this, male and female, of gold and of silver, have been found in quantity in Inca offerings. Most were made by joining two pieces of sheet metal at the sides of the figure. A seam can be seen here in the sides of the feet. At least some figures were dressed in specially made miniature garments, like dolls. Most examples have empty hands raised to the chest, although a few hold ears of maize. This one dangles an object like a fan. The Inca, who were fine engineers, technicians, and craftsmen, were sophisticated metallurgists, making alloys, like bronze, and inlaying silver and copper. Gold was associated with the sun, and the Inca emperor was considered to be the earthly incarnation of the sun. By law, the emperor controlled the distribution of gold and the wearing of gold ornaments. A great temple at Cuzco had walls sheathed in gold and a garden with maize plants and llamas of gold. These objects were collected for the ransom of the emperor Atahuallpa and melted down by the Spaniards.

INCA CULTURE. *Vessel, alpaca.*   *Below*

Small vessels in the form of alpacas or llamas provide some of the few examples of relatively realistic Inca sculpture. A number of these exist, undoubtedly made as vessels for offerings—there is a small hole in the back. This is a particularly attractive one. Effigies were also made of gold and silver. The alpaca, a camelid like the llama, but with longer, softer hair, was prized for its fur, as it is today. These animals graze on the great high plain that stretches from Cuzco to Tiahuanaco.

INCA CULTURE
Female figure
A.D. 1476–1534
Hammered gold; height *ca.* 10 cm.
Southern highlands (?)
The Gold Museum, Lima

Right
INCA CULTURE
Vessel, alpaca
A.D. 1476–1534
Stone; height 5 cm.
Southern highlands (?)

153

INCA CULTURE (?)
Warp-patterned tunic
Ca. A.D. 1400–1600
70×108 cm.
South coast
Obara-ryū Art Reference Museum

INCA CULTURE.   *Aryballoid vessel.*   *Facing page*

The most characteristic Inca ceramic shape, the aryballoid vessel, came in all sizes, finely made, highly fired, and decorated with abstract designs.   The vessel has a long neck with a flaring rim and two small loops for suspending decorative tassels; there is an animal head at the top of the rounded body of the vessel and a handle at each side; the base is conical.   This one is ornamented with a band of diamonds like a necktie.   Vessels of this form have been found from Ecuador to Chile.   The Inca had one of the most highly organized societies in the history of the world, and their force was felt over a much greater area than that of earlier people responsible for horizon styles.

Facing page
INCA CULTURE
Aryballoid vessel
A.D. 1476–1534
Polychrome ceramic; height 96 cm.
Southern highlands, Cuzco
Museum of the University of Cuzco

INCA CULTURE (?)   *Warp-patterned tunic.*

This multi-colored, striped tunic was probably made during Inca times, but it is not one of the official Inca tunics.   It is a warp-faced and warp-patterned textile—a construction technology which continues in the highlands of Peru to this day.   The patterned stripes use two-color complementary warp patterning, and the plain stripes are simply warp-faced.   The zig-zag selvedge binding on the right is characteristic of Late Horizon tunics, but the grouping of the stripes into three bands on each side seems reminiscent of the arrangement of earlier Middle Horizon tunics. The arrangement of colors in stripes is an ancient highland weaving art, and achieves great vibrancy and luminosity in this tunic, which may have been made in the highlands but was eventually buried on the coast. The warps are alpaca.

INCA CULTURE. *Flaring-rim vessel with jaguar handles.*

Jaguars and snakes still figure in the symbolic language of Inca art, even though most designs, like those on the body and rim of this vessel, are abstract. Effigy vessels have been replaced, however, by more utilitarian forms, except on the north coast (see p. 157). Quatrefoil patterns, like those seen in bands here, were popular, for the Inca called their empire "the world of the four quarters." The four world directions were generally important in Pre-Columbian cosmology.

Facing page
INCA CULTURE
Flaring-rim vessel with jaguar handles
A.D. 1476–1534
Polychrome ceramic; height 22 cm.
Southern highlands, Cuzco (?)
Museum of the University of Cuzco

INCA CULTURE
Spouted vessel, potato with monkey
A.D. 1476–1534
Burnished black ceramic; height 18 cm.
North coast
Amano Museum, Lima

INCA CULTURE.   *Spouted vessel, potato with monkey.*

The best potatoes in Peru come from some of the upper north-coast valleys, and the potato had long been reproduced in effigy ceramic vessels in that region. The monkey clutching the spout serves as a handle for this vessel. A small monkey on a spout had been a Chimú hallmark (see pp. 98, 110), and effigy monkey vessels had appeared in earlier north-coast ceramics. The blackware is also characteristic of the north coast. Although the imprint of the Inca art style is found all over their enormous empire, local styles and motifs still prevailed.

INCA CULTURE. *Beaker, or* kero.

The scene here shows a figure holding a large shield with his left hand and a staff or club with his right. At the viewer's left, a flowering plant seems to be used as a quiver. (The bow and arrow, the weapon of Amazon Basin tribes, was known in the highlands in the late period.) Similar flower forms are seen elsewhere on the vessel. Although the form of this vessel derives from the Tiahuanaco-Huari culture, and wooden beakers were common in the Inca period, this one must have been made just after the conquest. Pre-conquest wooden beakers were incised with abstract designs, but not painted. The framing of the upper-level scene, the drawing of the human figure, the shield, and the flower forms all suggest foreign influence. Many Pre-Columbian elements are preserved, however: the band of stepped-triangle design; the headdress; and the tunic, or *uncu*, with the stepped design at the neck, a garment motif that goes back at least to Mochica times.

INCA CULTURE
Beaker, or kero
Mid-16th century A.D.
Polychrome wood; height 20 cm.
Southern highlands (?)
Amano Museum, Lima

INCA CULTURE. *Beaker, or* kero, *jaguar head.*

The *kero* here becomes a snarling effigy jaguar head. Jaguar heads had been added to many kinds of vessels, but this is a new form. That the Inca recognized the symbolic power of large felines is attested by the fact that their capital, Cuzco, was conceived as a gigantic puma, partly natural and partly constructed. The legs straddled the ceremonial center, the tail was formed by two rivers meeting, and the head was outlined by the hilltop fortress of Sacsahuaman. A fierce feline head had been the defense of generations of Andean peoples.

INCA CULTURE. *Urn with animal handles.*   *p. 160*

This vessel relates to agricultural rituals, which were important in Inca times, and still are. At the time this urn was made, the traditional art of the Andes had encountered the art of Christian Spain, and a merging began which goes on until this day. The abstract designs are Inca; houses and plants have been shown on pottery throughout the Andes since early times; and Inca-period vessels show digging sticks like those seen below the house at the right. But the scenes with little figures, appearing under the digging sticks, reflect the Spanish influence that changed the Pre-Columbian world.

INCA CULTURE
Beaker, or kero, *jaguar head*
Mid-16th century
Carved and painted wood; height 22 cm.
Southern highlands, Cuzco (?)
Museum of the University of Cuzco

HISTORY OF ANDEAN ARCHAEOLOGY
AND MAP OF PERU

HISTORY OF ANDEAN ARCHAEOLOGY

The story of the origins and development of Andean archaeology begins with the earliest Spanish contact in 1524, and continues through the Colonial and Independence periods, leading at the close of the Early Republican period in 1900 to the emergence of the discipline of archaeology. It is to these three periods of time, spanning approximately 400 years, that we must look for the foundations of archaeology as it developed in this part of the South American continent.

THE CONQUEST AND COLONIAL PERIOD
(1524–1700)

During this period most chroniclers were Spanish, some were Italian, and others, at the end of the period, were Peruvian (either mestizo or Indian). They included soldiers, secretaries and government officials, but for the most part they were priests, missionaries, or friars. Matters of conquest and conversion account for the major occupations of the people involved.

Restrictions upon foreigners in the Spanish colonies explains why most of the chroniclers of the time were Spanish or people born in the colonies. These restrictions were enforced by the institution of the House of Trade and by antiforeign legislation, which created a monopoly of trade between Spain and the New World and controlled or excluded the travel of foreigners in the colonies. Furthermore, in 1570 the Inquisition and the Tribunal of the Holy Office were established to ensure that the colonies would be guarded from "dangerous thoughts" in religion, politics, and philosophy. Both these institutions were primarily aimed against foreigners. Publication and censorship of books were also controlled by the government.

Other factors which affected developments at this time included the Council of the Indies, the extirpation of idolatries, and the exploitation of the *huacas*, or sacred places. One function of the Council of the Indies (created in 1524) was to gather historical and geographical information (*relaciones*), an activity which was also carried on by the viceroys.

Methods of obtaining data mainly included direct observation, inquiries and interviews. For people in the sixteenth century, Inca sites and practices belonged to the time, and Indians had no difficulty identifying Inca sites if asked. But for pre-Inca archaeological remains the natives had only mythological explanations. Linguistic evidence was studied with the purpose of discovering New-World Indian origins; and as information accumulated some chroniclers (e.g., Cieza, Cobo, Garcilaso, and Guaman Poma) formulated syntheses.

Exploration was employed as a technique for locating and recording sites. With the uprooting of idolatries, objects from contemporary sites were more or less systematically described and the recording of such locations operated like an archaeological survey, although the purpose was drastically different—i.e., destruction of the objects for religious reasons.

With the exploitation of sacred places, or *huacas*, excavation was not perceived as a tool for resolving archaeological problems but for finding gold or silver. However, explicit bureaucratic regulations were established by the viceroy Francisco de Toledo: digging *huacas* required a license, having an inspector present, writing bimonthly reports, and registering everything found.

The first attempt to collect and preserve antiquities was made by Viceroy Toledo, who sent "Peruvian curiosities" to be incorporated into the king's museum at Madrid. The purpose was to preserve the remains of the conquered Incas and significant objects recovered from *huacas*. This coincided with the beginning of elite museums in Europe as royal collections housed in palaces; in addition to the royal museum at Madrid there was the Louvre, then a palace museum inaugurated in 1546. There is an interesting parallel between these and the Inca "elite museum" (*Puquin-Cancha*) in Cuzco, which was closed to all except the Inca and the imperial historians. Only certain persons were allowed access in each case, though in the late eighteenth century the Louvre was opened to the public.

Aside from description, the documentation of data included drawings, but these were exceedingly rare. Significantly, no maps and plans of archaeological sites were made.

However, cultural/ethnic classifications were established, and a theory of development or cultural evolution was developed. The comparative method (including linguistic comparisons) was employed, and a sense of what constituted acceptable scientific "evidence" and methodology began to emerge.

Of greatest importance was the work of the Jesuit Jose

de Acosta, who was among the most influential of this period. The American anthropologist John H. Rowe has argued in support of Acosta's contribution in developing a general hierarchical ethnological classification of non-Europeans, and a theory of cultural evolution that pre-dated the classic evolutionists of the nineteenth century by three hundred years. Acosta rejected the Atlantis, Ophirian, or any Transatlantic migration theory, as well as cultural or word comparisons as a means of demonstrating the origins of people in the Western Hemisphere. Instead, he used faunal and geographic arguments postulating a continuing land bridge, yet undiscovered and not based on European legend. Nevertheless, the Old World was ultimately seen as the place of origin, but an independent development was postulated for peoples once they arrived in the New World.

THE DECLINE OF COLONIALISM: INDEPENDENCE PERIOD (1700–1824)

A number of interrelated events occurred during this period which had a direct bearing on the development of Peruvian archaeology. The replacement of the last Spanish Habsburg king, Charles II, by Philip V, who belonged to the French Bourbon line, took place in 1700. As a result, French influence, especially as it related to the spread of the Enlightenment to Spain and the colonies, was significant. The Bourbons introduced new political and economic reforms, and sent viceroys and administrators with "French" ideas.

Under Bourbon rule also, the three major institutional restrictions, which had been strongly enforced in the previous period, declined and eventually came to an end at the close of the eighteenth century. These were: The House of Trade and the anti-foreign legislation, the decline of which for the first time allowed some foreigners to enter Spain and the colonies; the Council of the Indies, which had been in charge of the Spanish colonial government and controlled the Church (*Real Patronato*); and the Holy Office of the Inquisition.

In addition, the early scientific achievements in Europe outside of Spain gave rise to a new cultural climate in which aspects of human interest were subjected to the test of reason. This had major consequences for the development of Peruvian archaeology at this time: the theological paradigm was replaced by the principles of natural science, mainly as a result of the Enlightenment. The *philosophes* of the Enlightenment popularized rationalism and reason (even in disregard of Church and State authority), the abandonment of metaphysical explanations, reliance on empirical knowledge, and belief in the existence of universal laws of nature. With the emphasis on natural science, the enlightened Bourbon kings supported and financed scientific enterprises in the New World in order to find useful knowledge that could be applied to economy and industry. A greater interest in geography and cartography was motivated by political/territorial rearrangements and interest in trade. Furthermore, for the first time, some studies were undertaken for the sake of science alone. Museums gained support, collections were formed, the sciences developed in universities and schools, and foreign "experts" were called upon.

Within the context of these developments, it is easy to understand the variety of nationalities and professions represented among the precursors of Peruvian archaeology, their objectives in obtaining data, and the financing of their expeditions. In contrast to the previous period, only two Catholic officials were engaged in these enterprises, but both were trained in the natural sciences and one was a member of the French Academy of Sciences.

Political independence and the development of nationalism in Peru were crucial events that promoted additional developments in archaeology. In 1822, the year after José de San Martín declared the independence of Peru, the government issued a decree which, for the first time, demanded the protection of historical and archaeological monuments and called for the establishment of a National Museum. It stipulated that antiquities were the property of the nation, that their exportation was prohibited, and that their extraction required a government license.

The effects (direct and indirect) of the natural science paradigm on the development of Peruvian archaeology can be summarized as follows:

1. Antiquities became a legitimate subject for study, worthy of description and documentation in themselves, as reflected in the separate volumes devoted to them or in the illustrations solely of ruins or burials (e.g., Martínez de Compañon and Humboldt). Significantly, with José Hipólito Unanue the study of prehistoric remains was

163

regarded as a means of interpreting those cultures. Unanue used the term "paleosophy" to refer to what today is essentially regarded as archaeology. Also, out of nationalistic as well as "paleosophical" concerns, Unanue called for the study and preservation of archaeological remains.

2. With an emphasis on empirical observation, more accurate descriptions and documentation were produced. The first maps, plans, and measurements of ruins and a profile of excavation appeared in this period.

3. Speculation, though no longer within the premises of Christian theology, subsisted but diminished. Greater discipline and awareness of the need for documentation in interpretation developed. However, little interpretation occurred as yet; e.g., there was no further progress in terms of interpreting antiquity—only an Inca and a vague pre-Inca time were recognized.

4. Some scientific institutions arose which stimulated investigation, collecting and the preservation of ancient remains. Excavation (of burials) was used for the first time to collect antiquities for the public museums, and the periodical *Mercurio Peruano* provided a forum for the dispersal and exchange of knowledge.

5. Finally, as the interest in antiquities grew within the context of natural science, there were greater indications of a multidisciplinary approach, e.g., Unanue's use of "paleosophy" in conjunction with history and "ethnography," the beginning of ecology (Unanue and Humboldt), and first attempts at examining settlement patterns (Ulloa).

EARLY REPUBLICAN PERIOD (1824–1900)

This period begins with the year of the final defeat of Spanish rule and ends somewhat arbitrarily with the beginnings of industrialism in Peru, just before a discipline of archaeology began with Max Uhle. Peruvian independence and the rise of industrialism in Europe and the United States were the most significant foreign events influencing the development of Peruvian archaeology.

With independence, the doors of Peru were opened to foreigners and closed to Spaniards. As a newly created republic, Peru began developing its natural resources and trading with Europe and the United States, and consistently supported foreign immigration.

For the first time, in terms of the professions represented, no priests were involved in the development of archaeology. Rather, the Peruvian and foreign precursors of archaeology were now all either diplomats or natural scientists, with the sole exception of one military man. They all became involved in the study of archaeological remains in the process of establishing political or economic ties or in studying and assessing the exploitation of natural resources.

After the 1840's several interrelated developments occurred. First of all there was greater institutionalization, as indicated by the formation of societies, associations and museums. These institutions and their journals served to orient and sharpen the goals and methodology of the emerging discipline. They stimulated vastly increased collecting and most of the archaeological objects gathered at this time found their way to the newly created institutions. The formation of the National Museum in Peru in 1826 was largely the result of political and intellectual autonomy and nationalistic goals. Public interest and support were encouraged by the government, which also gave the first authorization for the formation of a "society" with the purpose of uncovering archaeological remains for the museum. Several private collections also were formed and sold in Europe and the United States. The Centeno Collection from Cuzco, for instance, was sold to the Ethnographic Museum of Berlin, where it later helped Max Uhle to become acquainted with the Inca style. In addition, the programs of modernization instituted by the Peruvian government—which were stimulated by foreign industrial needs for raw materials—led to the discovery of archaeological remains, and with that a profit-making motivation created large-scale looting and collecting. The process of discovery, then, had both detrimental and beneficial consequences for archaeology.

By the middle of the nineteenth century, archaeology and anthropology together came to be recognized as a discipline. The treatment of archaeological remains began to be regarded as a separate subject for study distinct from the natural sciences and related to anthropology. Entire books or articles solely on archaeology were written, including works by such scholars as the Peruvian natural scientist Mariano de Rivero and the Swiss explorer Johann Jakob von Tschudi.

Specialization and professionalism now developed. The

American Ephraim G. Squier has been regarded as the first specialized archaeologist of the whole American continent, although it may be pointed out that he came to Peru as the United States Commissioner appointed by Abraham Lincoln to mediate between the Peruvian government and the North American guano shippers. More exactly in this period, only Ernst Middendorf and Manuel Almagro can be considered true professionals in the sense of having been trained in archaeology/anthropology.

Regarding the methods used to obtain data, most if not all scholars of this period were multidisciplinary in their studies of ancient remains and peoples. These approaches included anthropology, history, and natural science. The end result was a more integral view of Peru, although for the most part archaeology remained a secondary concern. Direct empirical observation of archaeological, ethnographic, linguistic, and osteological aspects was then prevalent, as was exploration in varying degrees. Excavation greatly increased and for the first time photography was used in Peruvian archaeology.

By the end of this period, Inca, Tiahuanaco, and Chavín cultures and styles had been identified and partially defined; and the Colla, Chimú, and Recuay cultures had also been discussed. An even greater antiquity for lithic artifacts was postulated by several scholars, who remarked on the associations of extinct fauna with artifacts and human remains. Relative chronologies were proposed using evolutionary relationships of architecture, stone sculpture, and ornamental art.

Finally, as cultures came to be identified, so, too, did their geographic extension. For example, d'Orbigny argued that Samaypata (Bolivia) was the farthest Inca expansion toward the southeast; Markham defined the pre-Inca megalithic empire with its political and cultural center at Tiahuanaco as extending from Tucuman to the Marañón; and Middendorf's Chavín empire was also seen to have reached to the coast.

By the end of the nineteenth century, then, the foundations of Andean archaeology were well established. The major theoretical change that occurred in the eighteenth century, primarily as a result of the Enlightenment, was the substitution of a scientific approach for the theological paradigm which had prevailed in the seventeenth century. Speculation, description, analysis, and explanation were carried out in both periods, but in different degrees and with different objectives. The early twentieth century coincides with the emergence of Andean archaeology as a unified and scientific discipline, as well as an academic profession. In this emergence, the decisive influence of the German archaeologist Max Uhle marked the beginnings of new horizons in the search for understanding of the past.

THE MUSEUMS

As noted above, the National Museum of Anthropology and Archaeology was created by a government decree of April 2, 1822. On April 8, 1826, Mariano Eduardo de Riveroy Ustariz (a natural scientist, politician, and precursor of Peruvian archaeology) was appointed the first director. At that time the museum was known as the Museum of Natural History, Antiquities, History and Artistic Curiosities. It was originally located in a room of the old Inquisition quarters, and was affected by the prevailing political and economic instability of the time, to the point of once also becoming a storage place for school supplies.

In 1840 the museum was established more or less permanently in two rooms of the National Library, where it continued with the government's support and private donations. However, around this time the Swiss naturalist and explorer Johann Jakob von Tschudi visited the museum and noted that "it contains nothing of scientific value, and but for the series of historical portraits . . . it differs but little from the collections of curiosities frequently formed by amateurs. . ."

During the War of the Pacific and the Chilean occupation of Lima (1881), the National Museum was looted. The museum's holdings were taken to Chile, where they remain today at the Museum of Natural History of Santiago. In 1905 the museum was reestablished under a new name, Museo de Historia Nacional, with two sections—archaeology, under the direction of Max Uhle, and history. The archaeology section became independent in 1924 as the Museo de Arqueología Peruana, founded under the direction of Julio C. Tello, and incorporating the private collections of Victor Larco Herrera. Later in 1931 by government decree, the former Museo de Arqueología Peruana became the Museo Nacional with Luis E. Valcárcel as director, having Departments of History and of

Anthropology. A government decree of 1945 reorganized the museum in its present building as the National Museum of Anthropology and Archaeology. The twentieth century has seen the museum expand and modernize its extensive exhibits.

After 1900, regional museums were formed by local governments in various departments of Peru, or were founded by individuals with the holdings of large private collections. Examples of the former include the Museum and Archaeological Institute of the University of Cuzco, and the Regional Museum of Ica; while among the latter are the Rafael Larco Herrera Museum, the Amano Museum, and The Gold Museum, all in Lima. The Museum and Archaeological Institute of the National University of Cuzco began in 1848 as a museum and library located in the building of the old San Andrés Hospital of Cuzco. The Archaeological Institute was established in 1934 in commemoration of the fourth centenary of the founding of the City of Cuzco, and in 1941, this institute and the museum of the National University of Cuzco were brought together into the institution as it is known today.

This museum has some 10,000 objects comprising the departments of archaeology and history, and a specialized library. Over the years the collections have increased, thanks to private donations and archaeological surveys, making it the most important museum in the southern highlands of Peru.

The Regional Museum of Ica was founded by a government decree of March 30, 1947. This museum, located in the city of Ica, has some 12,000 objects, mainly obtained from private donations. Most pieces belong to the prehistoric cultures of the area, including Pre-ceramic, Paracas, Nasca, Huari, Ica, and Inca. Additional collections document the Colonial and Early Republican periods.

The Rafael Larco Herrera Museum was formed by the private initiative and efforts of the Larco family. In 1903, Rafael Larco Herrera, a Vice-President and Minister of Foreign Relations and Commerce of Peru, began a collection of North Coast ceramic vessels, which he subsequently donated to the Prado in Madrid. Then in 1925 Herrera began a new collection of archaeological objects acquired from his brother-in-law, Alfredo Hoyle. This became the basis for the Rafael Larco Herrera Museum, inaugurated in 1926 and housed in a building of the Chiclin hacienda, Chicama Valley. In subsequent years the collections were expanded by Herrera and later by his son Rafael Larco Hoyle and other members of the Larco and Hoyle families. Expeditions were made to different parts of Peru to obtain additional objects, and in 1933 two extensive collections were acquired: the Carranza collection from Trujillo, and the Roa collection from the Santa Valley—totaling some 11,000 objects. However, the major impulse came from Rafael Larco Hoyle, who, as an archaeologist, organized the collections and excavated in different areas of the north coast.

The family's agricultural business forced Rafael Larco Hoyle to move to Lima, and the Rafael Larco Herrera Museum was later brought to a colonial mansion in the capital city. Approximately 40,000 objects comprise its holdings and these are now officially registered as part of the national heritage of Peru. Among objects belonging to this museum studied and published by Rafael Larco Hoyle are the collections of erotic representations which were the object of particular interest for the sexologist Alfred C. Kinsey.

The Amano Museum was founded and organized by Yoshitaro Amano, a Japanese resident of Lima. His constant efforts over the years have led him to obtain an important collection of prehistoric textiles and ceramics, and to study their iconography. Most of the textile collections of this museum were extensively illustrated and published in 1957.

The well-known Gold Museum, containing collections of prehistoric Peruvian gold, silver, copper, textiles, featherwork, and jewelry, owed its beginnings to the private efforts of Miguel Mujica Gallo. Although the museum was established in 1966, already by the 1930's, Mujica Gallo was acquiring some of the most important items derived from lootings of ancient burials in the north coast. The collections, now registered as part of the national heritage of Peru, have been exhibited in different countries of South America, Mexico, the United States, Canada, and Europe.

Sergio J. Cháyez
Research Associate,
Institute of Andean Studies
Berkeley, California

EQUADOR

COLOMBIA

Napo River

Amazon River

Marañón River

Piura ● □ Vicus

BRAZIL

Batan Grande □
Lambayeque ●   □ Pacopampa

CHICAMA VALLEY
Cupisnique □

Cajamarca ●

Chanchan □ ● Trujillo
Moche □

VIRÚ VALLEY

Ucayali River

Huallaga River

Marañón River

Recuay ●
□ Chavín de Huantar

PERU

P
A
C
I
F
I
C

O
C
E
A
N

Chancay □

Lima ●

Apurímac River

Urubamba River

BOLIVIA

Chincha □

Huari □
Ayacucho ●

Machu Picchu □

Cuzco ●

Paracas □
Carowa □ ● Ica
Ocucaje □

Pacheco
Atarco □ □ ● Nasca

Lake
Titicaca

Tiahuanaco □ ● La Paz

0   100   200   300 Miles

0   100   200   300 Kilometers

CHILE

SELECTED BIBLIOGRAPHY

BENNETT, WENDELL C., AND BIRD, JUNIUS B. *Andean Culture History*. 2nd and revised edition. New York, 1964.

BENSON, ELIZABETH P. *The Mochica, a Culture of Peru*. Praeger Publishers, New York, 1972.

BUSHNELL, G. H. S. *Peru*. New York, 1957.

DISSELHOFF, HANS DIETRICH. *Daily Life in Ancient Peru*. New York, 1967.

KOSOK, PAUL. *Life, Land and Water in Ancient Peru*. New York, 1965.

LAPINER, ALAN. *Pre-Columbian Art of South America*. Harry N. Abrams, Inc., New York, 1976.

LUMBRERAS, LUIS G. *The Peoples and Cultures of Ancient Peru*. Transl. by Betty J. Meggers. Smithsonian Institution Press, Washington, D. C., 1974

LEHMANN, WALTER, AND DOERING, HEINRICH. *The Art of Old Peru*. London, 1924.

MORTIMER, W. GOLDEN. *Peru: History of Coca, the Divine Plant of the Incas*. New York, 1901.

OSBORNE, HAROLD. *South American Mythology*. London, 1968.

ROWE, JOHN HOWLAND. *Chavín Art: An Inquiry into its Form and Meaning*. The Museum of Primitive Art, New York, 1962.

SAWYER, ALAN. *Mastercraftsmen of Ancient Peru*. The Solomon R. Guggenheim Foundation, New York, 1968.

SQUIER, E. GEORGE. *Peru: Incidents of Travel and Exploration in the Land of the Incas*. New York, 1877.

STEVENSON, ROBERT. *Music in Aztec and Inca Territory*. Berkeley and Los Angeles, 1968.

TSUNOYAMA, YUKIHIRO. *Textiles of the Andes, Catalog of Amano Collection*. Heian/Dohosha, Tokyo, 1980.

UBBELOHDE-DOERING, HEINRICH. *The Art of Ancient Peru*. New York, 1954.

WARDWELL, ALLEN. *The Gold of Ancient America*. Museum of Fine Arts, Boston, The Art Institute of Chicago, and the Virginia Museum, 1968.

INDEX OF ILLUSTRATIONS

V LATE HORIZON PERIOD

INDEX OF NAMES

The numbers in italics refer to names cited in the captions

GENERAL INDEX